THE AMAZING
WORD OF GOD

I would recommend *The Amazing Word of God* to anyone who wants to gain some basic tools for understanding the Bible for themselves. Randy does a great job making the original Greek and Hebrew languages accessible to the average person and presenting key concepts for thorough study of the Word.

>Ross Nelson, Senior Pastor
>Northwoods Vineyard Church
>Tomahawk, Wisconsin

In Matthew, Jesus defeats the temptations of the devil by properly interpreting Scripture and by putting the focus back on God. Randy Fisk's book, *The Amazing Word of God*, gives people a set of easily understood tools to interpret God's Word properly, putting the focus on God in spite of temptations to do otherwise. May God use this clearly-written and useful book to increase the understanding of believers and to teach many to worship in Spirit and Truth.

>Jim L., Translator and Regional Director
>Wycliffe Bible Translators

THE AMAZING WORD OF GOD

SEMINARY-LEVEL INFORMATION
ANYONE CAN UNDERSTAND

RANDY FISK

LIBERTYVILLE, ILLINOIS

The Amazing Word of God—Seminary-Level Information Anyone Can Understand by Randy Fisk

Copyright © 2010 by Randy Fisk. All rights reserved.
This book may not be reproduced in any form for commercial gain or profit. Copying short quotations or occasional pages for personal or group use is encouraged. Otherwise seek the permission of the author.

Editor: Julie Pfitzinger
Cover Design: Laura Sebold
Book Layout: Mary Anne Pfitzinger

Published by This Joy! Books—A Division of Three Cord Ministries, Inc. 1117 S. Milwaukee Avenue, Suite A4, Libertyville, IL 60048

Distributed by Second Ref Press, North Aurora, Illinois 60542
www.secondrefpress.com

All Scripture quotations, unless otherwise indicated, are taken from the HOLY BIBLE, NEW INTERNATIONAL VERSION®. Copyright © 1973, 1978, 1984 Biblica. Used by permission of Zondervan. All rights reserved.

The "NIV" and "New International Version" trademarks are registered in the United States Patent and Trademark Office by Biblica. Use of either trademark requires the permission of Biblica.

Scripture noted "NKJV" is taken from the New King James Version. Copyright © 1982 by Thomas Nelson, Inc. Used by permission. All rights reserved.

The image of Matthew 13:14 from *Codex Sinaiticus* (p. 55) was printed with permission of the British Library, London, England.

The image of the Isaiah Scroll (p. 63), verse 7:14, a part of the *Dead Sea Scrolls*, was printed with permission of The Israel Museum, Jerusalem.

ISBN-13: 978-0-9821835-7-1
First printing, 2010
Printed in the United States of America

To my daughters:

Holly, Becky, and Mandy,

*and to my son-in-law,
Keith;*

and to their chosen generation.

ACKNOWLEDGMENTS

I would like to thank Mary, my wonderful wife, for helping and encouraging me, even when she did not realize she was doing so, as I developed and wrote this book. I would also like to thank my three daughters, Holly, Becky, and Mandy, and my son-in-law, Keith, for the ways God uses them and for being such inspirations to me.

I also appreciate my many friends, now and throughout the years, who have pointed the way toward my discovering more and more of God. I would especially like to single out the late Rev. Theodore Laesch, the pastor who led me to the Lord and whose heartfelt preaching gave me a love for the Word and for teaching it. I would also like to express my gratitude to my good friend, Rev. Dr. George Koch, to whom I am indebted for an abundance of insights and kindness.

I would like to thank Julie Pfitzinger for the wonderful touch she has in editing and her work with this book. I would also like to express my appreciation for Mary Anne Pfitzinger and everyone associated with This Joy! Books, who have been extraordinary to work with. And I would also like to thank my daughter, Mandy, for her encouragement and valuable suggestions as she poured over the manuscript in its early form.

And always, I would like to thank my Lord and God who always gives me more than I ask. Thank you for your amazing Word. I love you, everything you are, and forever will be.

CONTENTS

Introduction   p. ix

1 The Bible at First Glance   p. 1
2 Three Themes of the Old Testament   p. 5
3 Three Themes of the New Testament   p. 19
4 The Books of the Old Testament   p. 34
5 The Books of the New Testament   p. 42
6 Greek: The Language of the New Testament   p. 48
7 Hebrew: The Language of the Old Testament   p. 58
8 Systematic Theology   p. 65
9 How to Research the Word   p. 102
10 How to Teach the Word   p. 123
11 How to Apply and Enjoy the Word   p. 134

Appendix: Quizzes and Resources   p. 141
- Quizzes   p. 141
- Bibliography and Bible Study Resources   p. 147
- About the Author   p. 151

INTRODUCTION

About twenty-five years ago, shortly after my time at seminary, I set out to teach the leaders in our church the most important, interesting, and useful things I had learned in seminary. I called the course "Equipping the Equippers" and decided to make it somewhat like a college course since I was a university professor at the time. But I also wanted to make it move through the material quickly and be as practical as possible for those who would teach the Word themselves.

Since then, as I've continued learning about the Word, I've enhanced the material with information, insights, and heart attitudes that have proved invaluable to me. From all this, this book was written. As I've watched my own daughters grow up, I've wished to impart all I have learned to them and to their generation. So I've become increasingly inspired to write this material down for them to read and apply as they, in turn, touch the generations coming after them.

Seminaries tend to split the classes they offer into four major categories:

1. **Exegetical Theology** (Greek for *from the Word*):
   New Testament studies, Old Testament studies, the languages of the Bible

2. **Systematic Theology**: organizing the truths of the Bible into an orderly expression of its doctrines

3. **Practical Theology**: hermeneutics (how to give sermons), counseling, evangelism, worship, etc.

4. **Historical Theology**: the history of the church from Biblical times to recent days

I will follow a similar outline, although I will restrict myself to speaking about the Word and how to teach it. For this reason, my focus on historical theology, counseling, etc., will be brief.

It probably goes without saying that it is ridiculous, in one book, to attempt to cover more than a slim fraction of what is taught at a Christian seminary. A book of this size might be read in a day or two at a typical seminary. What I want to do, however, is write the things I learned that I wished I had known early on. I've always wondered why these things are taught only at the seminary level, yet I know they would be fascinating and extremely useful to the newest of believers as well as those who will be teaching others in their homes and classrooms.

My hope is that these chapters will be engaging to read through yet also good reference material to have on hand when needed. When looking at some of the chapters, such as those about Greek and Hebrew, please don't get frightened away thinking you could never learn such a language. I'm not teaching you to be fluent in these languages—I'm just giving you enough information which you will find interesting and will be useful when looking into individual words in a verse. At least wade into these chapters—you can always skip a section if you like.

It is my hope that you become equipped, be able to equip others, and find, as I have, the Word of God to be utterly amazing the more you look into its wondrous depths.

CHAPTER ONE

THE BIBLE AT FIRST GLANCE

Recently a friend of mine transferred a full-sized photograph of all the children of our church onto a wall next to the entrance of our church sanctuary. At first it seemed shocking—no one was used to seeing such a large photograph on the wall of a church. But after a month or two, I had become so used to its being there that, unless a newcomer commented on it, I barely noticed it. This is the way it is with anything new to us—once we grow accustomed to it, we forget our first impressions. That's also how it is with the Word of God. Those brought up in the church may never have had an unusual first impression of it. To others, our first impressions are barely a memory. Nevertheless, it is often useful to look at it as though it were the first time we read it. Not only do we gain insight into what newcomers to it might think, but it poses questions that can become gold mines of understanding for us—questions we might never think of asking once we have become accustomed to the Word.

Forgive me if the description I am about to give of a person's possible first impression of the Word sounds a bit irreverent. But you have to admit that the Bible is a rather unusual book! However, we will find that the very ways in which it is unusual are, in fact, tailor-made to the amazing message, themes, and purposes running throughout its pages.

So let's pretend we have never set eyes on the Bible before and consider it anew.

CHAPTER 1

FIRST IMPRESSIONS

Consider this. A billion is about as high as you can count. (If you counted once per second, night and day, it would take thirty-two years.) A trillion is a thousand times that. There are about one hundred billion galaxies in the universe, the largest of which is three times bigger than our own galaxy and contains a trillion stars. The entire universe contains thirty to seventy billion trillion stars. Each star is mind-bogglingly massive—our sun weighs a thousand trillion trillion tons. Looking at the world microscopically is equally as mind-boggling. In the diamond of a typical wedding ring there are a trillion trillion carbon atoms. All in all, there are a hundred million trillion trillion trillion trillion trillion trillion atoms in the universe, amazing in its diversity whether we are looking at the level of atoms, cells, human beings, waterfalls, solar systems, or galaxies. Who is this God who created it all? If he were to write a book, what do you suppose it would be like?

If you had never heard of the Bible and someone were to tell you that God had written a book, you probably would imagine that it must be a very orderly account covering every aspect of God: God is all-powerful, God is kind, God is just, and so forth. In other words, you would expect it to be like a *theology* book.

If you were to open the Bible for the first time, however, you would be in for a surprise. You would find lots of stories, many of them about people whose behavior casts them in a very unflattering light. People, even the good guys, often did things which must have made them a little ashamed when they showed up in God's book.

For example, King David is one of the heroes of the book. Yet there is a story about David having an affair with Bathsheba—a married woman. And then, to cover it up, he saw to it that her husband, one of his most devoted warriors, was put into harm's way and lost his life. Now why would God put *that* in his book?

Then there are all the genealogies. Why would God be interested in genealogies? Why should we be interested in the names of all those fathers, grandfathers, and fathers of the grandfathers? We thought we were going to learn about God, not about people.

If we were to tell someone about our strange impression of the Bible, they might say, "You should have started with the New Testament, not the Old Testament." So we excitedly turn to Matthew 1, the first chapter of the New Testament, only to find . . . more genealogy!

Granted, even at first glance, we find some astonishingly good things in the Bible, too. Amazing things. But why all the weird things, like people's experiences and genealogies?

> Once we start looking at what the Bible is all about, we will find there are profound reasons why it is the way it is.

Once we start discovering what the Bible is all about, we will find there are profound reasons why it is the way it is. It is, in fact, tailor-made to convey its themes and purposes. Once we see this, we will realize that no one would have sat down to write a book like this in their own humanity. If you wanted to write your own book and say God wrote it, you would not make yourself or your friends look so bad. No one in their right mind would do that. The only answer that makes sense is that it really is God's book. When we start seeing the reasons why it is written the way it is, we will see that God wrote it with a passion—a passion that its words would come alive as we and countless others read it—a passion that we would become transformed by him as we begin to know him. In it we will also discover our destiny in him, which is far beyond what we could think or imagine.

So let us start looking at what God put in his book.

CHAPTER 1

Thinking More About It

Ω Read some of the Bible pretending you are reading it for the first time. Note some things that might seem odd to a first-time reader.

Ω Try to guess what the themes of the entire Old Testament are. See if the next chapter agrees with what you thought.

CHAPTER TWO

THREE THEMES OF THE OLD TESTAMENT

I've heard many teachers talk about the themes of certain books or passages of the Bible, but this chapter is going to talk about the themes of the entire Old Testament itself. These are the major themes that thread their way through the Old Testament and, as we will see in the next chapter, are picked up again in the New Testament. It is important to keep these in mind when we focus on particular passages in Scripture, because the individual passages always fit into the tapestry of a bigger picture and often tie into the grand themes that God is trying to convey. Recognizing these themes will shed light on all we talk about when looking into the amazing Word of God.

There are a number of themes that wind their way through the Old Testament, but I find these three to be the major ones:

   I. **Knowing God**
   II. **The Promised Messiah**
   III. **Living as God's People**

Although some may express these differently or add others to the list, I find them fairly clear choices. Certainly God wants to reveal who he is. And it is quite apparent that a majority of the Old Testament is about his interaction with people and the way he wanted them to live. As for the second theme, some very central Old Testament texts speak about the Messiah, and that has been a major theme in Judaism throughout its history.

CHAPTER 2

I. KNOWING GOD

Much of the Old Testament is written so that we may know God. This is not surprising—God wrote his book so that we would know who he is. But it goes beyond giving us information *about* God. Its intent is that we would actually come to *know* him—personally.

If it truly is God's intent, in writing the Bible, that we know him, how does he do that? Perhaps we should begin by asking ourselves, how do we get to know any person?

Knowing about God

The first way we get to know a person is by knowing about him. We could do this by hearing other people tell us what that person is like, or we could gather this information from the person himself. Certainly the Bible has a lot of information about God. Early on God tells Moses his name is "I Am," or in Hebrew, "Yahweh" (Exodus 3:14). As time goes on, God reveals more and more about himself, often by giving himself more names, such as "Yahweh of hosts" (1 Samuel 17:45), "Yahweh who heals" (Exodus 15:26), or "Yahweh who provides" (Genesis 22:14).

Spending Time with Him

We also get to know a person by spending time together. Certainly the Bible is filled with instances of how delighted God was with those who loved to spend time in his presence, displaying how wide his heart is to spend time with us as well. The sheer length of the Bible suggests the abundance of opportunity and desire on his part to spend time with us.

Sharing Experiences with Him

We also get to know people by sharing experiences. That's when we really see what people are like. I once heard a family counselor talk about the most powerful ways a family can bond to one another. At the top of his list was the sharing of experiences. He claimed that often the worst experiences provided the most opportunities for bonding. For example, maybe there was a doomed camping trip where, in the midst of a downpour, the tent slipped down a hill with the family inside! Unless the family were to fall victim to anger and self-pity, they may often remember how much they were shaking that night and laugh as they recall the expressions they saw on each other's faces, knowing now that they can survive a storm together. The experience has the potential to bond them closely together for life.

So it is with God. We can know about God, but when the rubber meets the road and we travel with him over the best or worst parts of our lives—when we see him faithful, merciful, or providing in unexpected ways—then we come to know him as never before and are increasingly bonded together.

We do learn about God through facts about him, but facts about him can become a greater part of us when illustrated by experience. This can happen not only through our own experiences with God, but also in hearing about the experiences of others.

> Facts about God can become a greater part of us when illustrated by experience.

Part of what is called the "Hebrew mind-set" is a slightly different approach to gaining knowledge. In the West, we tend to migrate toward a rational approach to knowledge. The Hebrew (or Eastern) mind-set of the people to whom the Bible was originally written leans a little more heavily on gaining knowledge through experience. For example, someone once asked people from the West this question: "If cotton only grows in warm climates and England has a cold climate, does cotton grow in England?" The majority of people in the West instantly answered, "If England has a cold climate, then, of course, cotton wouldn't grow there." However, in the East a typical response was, "I don't know; I've never been to England." To us in the West, that answer sounds strange. However, if our first approach to knowledge were experience, we might answer such questions by first looking at what we've experienced. This does not mean that either approach to knowledge is wrong. Actually both are important. Experience has a way of illustrating a truth and, because of the way we were made, it knits that truth deep inside us.

God knows this and has actually provided both ways of presenting truth in Scripture. There is the more logical, rational approach, such as we find in Paul's letters. But there are also many accounts of people's experiences for us to learn from, which is why the Bible is filled with so many stories. For God to tell us that he has a heart to forgive us is one thing, but to illustrate this in the way he forgave David for all the wrongs surrounding the Bathsheba incident is quite another. It is God's desire that we not only know facts about him, but that those facts be placed deep within us and form a bond that would resonate in both our heads and hearts. It is interesting that Jesus often taught using parables (simple stories or illustrations), usually without even directly stating the truth they illustrated! He desires for us to dig out the truths and let the parables impact our hearts as we ponder them in our minds.

God has given us his Word so that we may place ourselves into the shoes of the original hearers—or even into his shoes—and let the stories impact us as we hear them. So, as God reveals who he is by giving us his names, such as "Yahweh who provides," he also relates stories of what people went through as they discovered just how much he really is the God who provides.

Not only do we learn about God through stories (by "stories" I mean true accounts) in Scripture, but he gives us our own stories as we walk through life with him. That is our God at work. This does not mean, however, that our personal belief systems should be forged solely through our personal experiences. There is danger in that. If taken wrongly, we could react with bitterness and hopelessness to negative experiences, or we could react with egotism to positive ones. The great thing about the stories in Scripture is that they also show us the right way to react to them and the lessons to be learned. Only after we have those things in our hearts, can we see how the Author of Life is expecting us to react and grow through our own life experiences. That is the time when our experiences can bond us to him in the ways he has intended.

Intimacy with God

Scripture shows us that to know God is vital. Jesus will say to those he rejects, "I don't know you . . ." (Luke 13:27). Knowing God is what will help us to be strong in the end times: "But the people who know their God shall be strong, and carry out great exploits" (Daniel 11:32, NKJV). But what all is involved in knowing him? As I said before, it is more than knowing *about* God—God's heart is for us to know him personally.

Actually, the word "know" in Scripture (the Hebrew word is *yada*) even goes beyond knowing about or knowing personally—it can also denote intimacy. When Genesis 4:1 says that Adam knew (*yada*) Eve and they conceived a child, the reference was to physical intimacy. The knowing of God, then, also includes bringing us into a spiritual intimacy. But how do we do this?

Sharing the Secrets of Our Hearts

One road to intimacy is through sharing the secrets of our hearts. Years ago, just after a rash of pastors had fallen into immorality, our area overseer brought his pastors together to teach us how this can happen in order to prevent any of us from heading in that direction. The overseer told us that it usually does not happen because we see an unusually beautiful woman and cannot resist the physical attraction. Usually the way it happens is that, in our counseling, we hear the secrets of a woman's heart and then start sharing with her the secrets of our hearts—something we should do only with our spouses. What we often don't realize is that there is a strong bonding that can happen as we share the secrets of our hearts. Once this strong bond develops, taking the step into physical intimacy can occur all too easily.

In hearing this, I began to think that if the sharing of our hearts can develop bonding in a negative way, then could the increased sharing of hearts with our spouses enhance bonding in a good way? I tried it. The answer was yes! I would highly recommend taking time to share those secrets—your innermost dreams and fears—with your husband or wife. It truly does bring bonding and intimacy.

> One road to intimacy is through sharing the secrets of our hearts.

If this is true with people, is it true with God? It most certainly is, and God uses it to bring us into intimacy with himself. In Scripture, he shares with us his innermost desires, dreams, and even emotions. We also see the heroes of the faith, such as Moses, David, and many of the prophets sharing these things with him. They are examples for us to follow. He truly wants for us to share our innermost secrets with him. And he will impress his innermost secrets upon us. In doing so, our intimacy with him will grow.

Transparency

When Adam and Eve fell, one victim of the Fall was their intimacy with God. It is interesting that one of the first things they did was to clothe themselves. Spiritually we can do the same thing—we can reach out to anything that would hide us from being vulnerable or transparent with God. Whether it is excuses for what we do, presenting a false face over what we feel, or an aura of self-importance, we grab for it and are so used to it being there that we soon do not even know ourselves. So one step toward intimacy with

God is to remove those things we are using to cover our inner selves and desire to be open and transparent before him. Only when we have a heart to do this can we be open and transparent before others.

As I mentioned before, this is exactly the heart that was in the heroes of God, such as Moses and David. And that is part of the reason these people were willing to look so bad in God's book. They cared more about being open with, right with, and close to God than they cared about what anyone else thought. They would rather cry out, "Search me, O God, and know my heart," (Psalm 139:23) than look good to others.

Loving God

As we can see, God wrote his Word so that we may know him. Even beyond that, it is written that we would come near to him and love him. It is a desire he spoke to Moses (Deuteronomy 6:5). It is exemplified in David's psalms (Psalm 18:1). The Psalms are actually worship, which is a beautiful way of expressing our love to God intimately. God's heart is that we would be drawn into loving him out of knowing who he is and discovering his amazing love for us (Jeremiah 31:3).

> God has laid out in his Word a path that we all may know him.

Opening the Bible in order to know about God is good, but once we get into what he has written, we are in for far more than that. He has laid out in his Word a path that we all may know him . . . be bonded to him . . . know him personally . . . love him. And this process will not leave us unchanged. It is comparable to falling in love with another person. We are changed from the inside out, and our innermost desire—which drives what we think and do—becomes, "I want to know God more." This knowing and loving God is an underlying theme weaving its way throughout the pages of the Old Testament. It will weave its way into the New Testament as well.

CHAPTER 2

II. THE PROMISED MESSIAH

Another prominent theme in the Old Testament is the promised Messiah. It begins with the Promised Seed spoken about after the fall of Adam and Eve in Genesis 3:15, "And I will put enmity between you and the woman, and between your seed and her Seed; he shall bruise your head, and you shall bruise His heel" (NKJV). From that point on came the expectation of the descendant (the Seed) of whom this verse spoke. Generation after generation, the people wondered if this was the time he would come. First they learned he would descend from Abraham. Then from Judah. Then from David. No wonder the repeated emphasis on genealogy in Scripture! The Descendant was to come, and Scripture became more and more specific.

Note: For thousands of years, the Jewish people believed that the coming Messiah was to be a person. Even today, many Orthodox Jews believe this. However, many leaders of modern Judaism now teach that the Messiah refers to the Jewish people as a whole. One might think that this shift in thinking came about in reaction to Christianity. That, however, is not the case. The idea came in AD 135. At that time Akiva was the prominent teacher in Israel. Akiva was the head of the rabbinical school in Jamnia, the school which had been in Jerusalem until the destruction of the Temple in AD 69. (When Jesus was young, Hillel was leader of that school.) Akiva, like his predecessors, believed the Messiah was a person. In fact, Akiva announced that a contemporary of his, a Jewish military hero named Bar Kokhba, was the Messiah. This was because Bar Kokhba overthrew the chains of Rome starting in AD 132 and Akiva thought that is what the Messiah was supposed to do. All was well until Rome (under Hadrian) had enough of this and sent an army which annihilated Bar Kokhba and his troops and put Israel back under Rome and suffering. Due to the bloody and horrific defeat, the scholars at Jamnia decided that it was best not to predict any more Messiahs—the idea led to too much suffering and heartbreak for the people. So they changed their interpretation of the Messiah from being an individual to being the Jewish people themselves. However, this is at odds with centuries of Jewish Scriptural interpretation and writings. The Talmud (a book of revered rabbinic writings) talks about the Messiah as a person. It says that when the Messiah comes, if the people are meritorious, then he will come with the clouds of heaven; otherwise he will come lowly and riding upon a donkey (Sanhedrin 98a). (It's interesting that we believe that both interpretations are right—he has or will come in both ways!) [Many thanks to Rev. Dr. George Koch for his research on these Messianic expectations.]

In the Old Testament, the Messianic references are many. Here are a few:

- *In your seed all the nations of the earth shall be blessed, because you have obeyed My voice.* (Genesis 22:18, NKJV)

- *He said to me, "You are my Son, today I have become your Father. Ask of me, and I will make the nations your inheritance,". . . Kiss the Son, lest he be angry and you be destroyed in your way.* (Psalm 2:7,12)

- *The LORD says to my Lord: "Sit at my right hand until I make your enemies a footstool for your feet."* (Psalm 110:1)

- *Therefore the LORD himself will give you a sign. The virgin will be with child and will give birth to a son, and will call him Immanuel* [which means God with us]. (Isaiah 7:14)

- *For unto us a Child is born, unto us a Son is given; and the government will be upon His shoulder. And His name will be called Wonderful, Counselor, Mighty God, Everlasting Father, Prince of Peace.* (Isaiah 9:6, NKJV)

- *"The days are coming," declares the LORD, "when I will raise up to David a righteous Branch, a King who will reign wisely. . . . This is the name by which he will be called: The LORD Our Righteousness."* (Jeremiah 23:5–6)

- *But you, Bethlehem Ephrathah, though you are small among the clans of Judah, out of you will come for me one who will be ruler over Israel, whose origins are from of old, from ancient times.* (Micah 5:2)

- *"See, I will send my messenger, who will prepare the way before me. Then suddenly the Lord you are seeking will come to his temple; the messenger of the covenant, whom you desire, will come," says the LORD Almighty.* (Malachi 3:1)

There are also a number of prophecies foreseeing the Messiah's suffering and death. Isaiah 53 is a remarkable chapter, describing this in great detail. Not only that, but it declares the reason for it:

Surely he took up our infirmities and carried our sorrows, yet we considered him stricken by God, smitten by him, and afflicted. . . . For he bore the sin of many, and made intercession for the transgressors. (Isaiah 53: 4, 12b)

This passage and others give specific details about the Messiah's suffering. Isaiah 53:9 tells us that he will be buried with the rich. Zechariah 12:10 and Psalm 22:16 say he will be pierced. If you haven't already, read these texts (including all of Isaiah 53) for yourself—their impact needs to be felt as you read them.

There are prophecies, such as Isaiah 53, which describe the Messiah's coming as a suffering servant and others, such as Daniel 7:13–14, which describe his coming as a conquering king. Hearing the words when they were spoken, it was not always clear that these were referring to two separate events. With New Testament eyes we can see these are describing his first and second comings. However, back when the prophecies were given, these Messianic glimpses have been likened to seeing two mountains in the distance. If you have ever approached a mountain range, you know that two mountains often look like one until you have arrived at a place between them. Therefore, the eyes of the prophets often went from one mountain to the other and back again, describing what they were seeing without distinguishing the actual sequence of events. We are now at a time when we can tell one mountain from the other because one is behind us and the other is ahead.

As the people of the Old Testament longed to see the fulfillment of the promised Messiah, we, too, need to capture this longing. Even though we have found him, the Old Testament is a constant reminder of the wonder of it all.

III. LIVING AS GOD'S PEOPLE

As prophesies unfolded describing what lineage the Messiah would come from, we can see that God had chosen a people to watch. Not only were these people chosen to be ancestors to the Messiah, however—God also loved them and chose them to show the world how a people belonging to him should live.

Note: This is not to say God didn't love the rest of the world. He did. A sizable portion of the prophetic books are directed to the other nations. In Genesis 22:18 God promised to Abraham: "In your seed all the nations on earth shall be blessed" (NKJV). God's heart for the nations is another theme that winds through Scripture. It, like the other themes, has a remarkable fulfillment in the New Testament.

In the first five books of the Bible, the major portion is about Israel, chosen by God, and about the law, telling Israel how to live as God's people. Through Moses, God expressed in clear terms how people should behave, giving laws describing what they should do and

> There was cycle after cycle of obedience, sin, consequences of sin, repentance, and restoration.

not do. The law was good, useful, and wonderful, written for the good of the people. Living up to the law proved easier said than done, however.

There was some success in living as God desired, but a lot of failure. (The Bible is remarkable in its openness about this.) There was cycle after cycle of obedience, sin, consequences of sin, repentance, and restoration. This continued, in different forms, throughout the history of Israel, from the time of Moses to the time when the last word was penned in the Old Testament. But were God's people meant to go through these cycles? Are we, ourselves, trapped in them? Do we try to be good, fail, come back, fail, and repeat this process over and over again? As Paul said in Romans 7:22–24:

For in my inner being I delight in God's law; but I see another law at work in the members of my body, waging war against the law of my mind and making me a prisoner of the law of sin at work within my members. What a wretched man I am! Who will rescue me from this body of death?

Isn't there a better way?

THREE THEMES LEFT UNFULFILLED

The Old Testament ends with each of its themes crying out for more. Intimacy was lost in the Garden of Eden—it had not been fully restored. The Messiah had been promised but had not yet come. The people tried to obey, but failed again and again—the Old Testament ends with them still in one of these cycles.

The Old Testament spoke of something more to come. Jeremiah 31:33–34 (NKJV) says this:

But this is the covenant that I will make with the house of Israel after those days, says the LORD: I will put My law in their minds, and write it on their hearts; and I will be their God, and they shall be My people. No more shall every man teach his neighbor, and every man his brother, saying, 'Know the Lord,' for they all shall know Me, from the least of them to the greatest of them, says the LORD. For I will forgive their iniquity, and their sin I will remember no more.

Here it is: a promise of knowing God, and of writing the law inside our hearts. Yet the Old Testament ends with this promise yet to come. It ends with the Messiah still on the way.

> "For they all shall know me, from the least of them to the greatest of them, says the LORD."

Who would write a book with all of its themes unresolved? Would the perfect God do that? No author I know would do that unless another book (or Testament) were on the way.

CHAPTER 2

Thinking More About It

Ω Read some of the Bible putting yourself in the shoes of the original hearers, of the people in the stories, and even of God. Read some of the dialogue out loud, trying to inflect the words in the way they might have been spoken.

Ω Review the three themes mentioned in this chapter. Though they are major themes, the list of themes is not exhaustive. Try thinking of some more.

Ω Consider whether these themes of the Old Testament might possibly be applicable to the New Testament. See if the next chapter agrees with what you thought.

CHAPTER THREE

THREE THEMES OF THE NEW TESTAMENT

The three themes of the Old Testament discussed in the last chapter, having been left mostly unfulfilled, continue on as major themes in the New Testament where they are fulfilled in surprising ways. The New Testament is about the life and ministry of the Messiah—born of the lineage of Abraham and David in the town of Bethlehem—Jesus of Nazareth. Who he was and what he did is the dominant theme in the New Testament. It is the root from which the other two themes are fulfilled.

I. THE PROMISED MESSIAH

Four hundred years elapsed between the last word written in the Old Testament and the birth of Jesus. This does not mean God was inactive during those years. During that time, the Greek empire had given way to the Roman conquest of a large part of the world including Israel and its surrounding lands. The Greeks had left behind their language, which remained universally spoken in the expansive Roman empire, while Roman ships and roads brought about transportation more rapid than the world had ever known. God, as the author of history, had seen to it that a common language and fast transportation could spread the message of the coming Messiah like never before. In fact, such a phenomenon involving language and transportation has only been known twice in the history of the world—once in that day and the other in our day, with English now being so universally known.

More than four hundred years before the birth of Jesus, the Old Testament prophet Daniel recorded some strange words which foretold the time of the Messiah:

> *Know and understand this: From the issuing of the decree to restore and rebuild Jerusalem until the Anointed One [Messiah], the ruler, comes, there will be seven 'sevens,' and sixty-two 'sevens.' It will be rebuilt with streets and a trench, but in times of trouble. After the sixty-two 'sevens,' the Anointed One will be cut off.* (Daniel 9:25–26a)

The decree to restore Jerusalem was almost certainly the one made by the Persian king Artaxerxes in 444–445 BC. Prophetically, days often represented years. So these sixty-nine (the first seven plus latter sixty-two) "sevens" until the Messiah would be cut off ("cut off" is a euphemism for "killed") would then have represented 483 years. That would put the death of the Messiah at AD 38–39. If one day represented a strict Levitical year of 360 days (twelve thirty-day months), however, this would put it at AD 31–32 which is, in fact, the date of the crucifixion of Jesus. That is a rather remarkable coincidence (unless God planned it that way)!

As mentioned in chapter 1, the New Testament opens with the genealogy of Jesus (Matthew 1:1–16). The message of Matthew beginning this way is clear—this theme, this longing to see the coming of the Messiah, which runs throughout the Old Testament, was now complete. At the time of God's choosing, the Messiah had come. As to exactly what he would be like, the people were in for some surprises, even though those surprises had been prophesied all along.

THREE THEMES OF THE NEW TESTAMENT

The Suffering Servant vs. Conquering King

For two reasons, the religious leaders of Jesus' day expected the Messiah to come as a conquering king. First, as previously mentioned, the Old Testament prophets often described the first coming of Jesus (as the suffering servant) and the second coming (as the conquering king) as if they were one event, not two. Second, the Roman occupation of Israel produced a longing for a return to the prosperous, independent kingdom of Israel that had flourished centuries before. If the Roman occupation was a punishment for Israel's disobedience, the Jewish leaders felt they were now going overboard in their obedience to the law, so there was no reason why the Messiah should not step in and lead Israel back to freedom and prosperity. That is what God had done so many times before when Israel had turned and obeyed him. So would the Messiah really come this time as a conquering king? Yes and no.

When Jesus came, in some respects he was both a suffering servant and conquering king. The conquering-king aspects of his first and second comings, of course, are quite different—in his second coming his overwhelming presence will cause all to bow before him, some willingly and some unwillingly. But establishing a kingdom in order to conquer the world is actually what he did in his first coming, as well. How he did this was the first of many surprises.

> His immediate aim was not to conquer Rome. He came to conquer a far worse enemy.

Jesus came as the point man of a heavenly invasion. However his immediate aim was not to conquer Rome. He came to conquer a far worse enemy than that. And he did not come just to restore Israel's political kingdom; he came to bring us into a kingdom where we would know hope, life, freedom, and light—no political institution could even come close to providing this.

CHAPTER 3

The kingdom he came to conquer was the kingdom of the enemy: Satan's kingdom, to which our own sin had given him the keys. That kingdom was characterized by darkness, deceit, death, disease, and every kind of bondage. Jesus came to show that his Kingdom had come, characterized by just the opposite: light, truth, life, wholeness, and freedom. His words described this Kingdom; his works demonstrated that the reality of it was here.

This Kingdom he brought would come in a very personal and caring way. Anything political or self-promoting was simply incongruent with the nature of this Kingdom. This, however, made the Kingdom easy to miss for those who expected the world's type of conquering king. It was God's plan to draw us through our hearts, not our eyes or worldly-minded heads.

> **The Kingdom Jesus brought would come in a very personal and caring way.**

The term "Kingdom of God" (or "Kingdom of heaven") is used 104 times in the New Testament, mostly in Matthew, Mark, and Luke. Often Jesus spoke of the Kingdom of God in parables. As mentioned before, these parables did not spoon-feed the truth, but rather drew hungry hearts to himself through illustrations and Spirit-enabled discovery. Some of these parables described the goodness of the Kingdom. Some, like the parable of the prodigal son (Luke 15:11–32), described how the Father's heart was longing for the return of his children. Many parables, however, described the growth of the Kingdom and how easy it is to miss it when its beginnings are as small as a mustard seed.

Every action of Jesus was clothed in humility. He had a humble birth where he was laid in a feeding trough and wrapped in swaddling cloths—reminiscent of the cloths that would wrap his body after the lowliest of deaths. In his ministry he resisted any efforts to give him worldly glory or the promotion of man. Being humble, however, did not mean he didn't exhibit boldness and strength. He exhibited both in great measure. Boldness goes hand in hand with humility; boldness and humility are the opposites of pride and insecurity, of which Jesus had none. He was also strong (Revelation 5:5). The very fact that he endured the suffering he went through prior to his death showed he had great strength, which he always used for our good, not his.

The Anointed One and Immanuel

Jesus was the Messiah (*mashiach*), Hebrew for "Anointed One." (The Greek word is *Christos,* from which we get Christ.) In other words, he was anointed and filled with the Holy Spirit.

Another surprise is that not only would he be anointed by God, but he would *be* God. The Old Testament bears this out: his name would be *Immanuel* (Isaiah 7:14), meaning "God with us." The New Testament bears this out as well: it continues the revelations of the "I Am" names ("I Am" is what *Yahweh* means in Hebrew), now directed at Jesus: "I am the good shepherd" (John 10:11) and "I am the way, the truth, and the life" (John 14:6, NKJV). In one of his rare confessions of who he was to the Jewish leaders, Jesus said, "Before Abraham was, I AM" (John 8:58, NKJV). They understood the implications of what he was saying and tried to stone him for it. And finally, when being arrested before his death and asked if he was Jesus, he answered, "I am He" (John 18:5, NKJV), at which point the soldiers and officials fell to the ground at the uncontainable power of this word.

"I AM."

In his humility, however, Jesus even laid down the recognition of the fact that he was God:

> *Your attitude should be the same as that of Christ Jesus: who, being in very nature God, did not consider equality with God something to be grasped, but made himself nothing, taking the very nature of a servant, being made in human likeness, and*

being found in appearance as a man, he humbled himself and became obedient to death—even death on a cross! (Philippians 2:5–8)

This is the way in which he ministered—he set aside exhibiting his divine nature, yet was filled and anointed with the Holy Spirit, walking in humility yet power (Luke 4:14). In doing this, he became an example of how we, too, are to minister and live.

The Lamb of God

Jesus was the ultimate suffering servant. Even though Isaiah had foretold, "Who has believed our message and to whom has the arm of the LORD been revealed?" (Isaiah 53:1) and then went on to describe his agony and death for our atonement, no one could have guessed that the sacrificial lambs of the Old Testament foreshadowed something the Messiah would do. He actually became God's lamb of sacrifice for us all. But, then again, no one could have guessed the trouble we were really in and that the only answer was a lamb so perfect, so holy, so close to God's own heart, that it took his only begotten Son to be our sacrifice.

This was not only a surprise for the people of his day, but there are aspects of it which continue to be a surprise to us. As we see the beauty of this Son in the Word, as we get to know him, as we watch him live and talk and minister, it becomes more and more unthinkable that our own sin should mar this one of beauty. But the Bible goes beyond this in incomprehensibility—it says he *became* sin (2 Corinthians 5:21).

> "My God, my God, why have you forsaken me?"

We see similar descriptive language in John 3:14 when Jesus likened himself to the snake (which always represented sin) that Moses raised up on the pole, so that when the Israelites gazed upon that which had bitten them, they would be made well. However, we know that "sin" and "God" simply do not mix—1 John 1:5 says there is no darkness in God whatsoever. So how could God the Son become sin? That is, indeed, a mystery, but true. When Jesus took sin upon himself (our sin), God the Father had to turn away. He could have no fellowship with sin. He had to listen to the Son he loved cry out, "My God, my God, why have you forsaken me?" (Matthew 27:46). In Jesus' time of need, the Father had to turn from him. The physical aspect of Jesus' death was terrifying, but the spiritual suffering, the separation from his Father whom he had always loved and known, must have been even more so. Yet he did it. And for one reason. For us. If you ever wonder if God loves you, look at this. The extent of his suffering is the extent of his love for us. For you. For me. For us all.

II. LIVING AS GOD'S PEOPLE

What had happened on the cross is what I call the **great exchange**. Jesus went to the cross with no sin, deserving nothing but goodness and life forever with God. We, on the other hand, were found filled with sin, deserving punishment and separation from God. Somehow we ended up with what Jesus deserved; he ended up with what we deserved.

The struggle to live as God pleases suddenly took a surprising turn. Because of what happened on the cross, we were declared righteous without actually having earned it. Righteousness was given by God's grace and by nothing we have done or could do. Was God out of his mind when he did this? Did he suddenly give up on us living as we should and say, "Oh well!"? Would this actually have an effect on the way we live?

> The struggle to live as God pleases suddenly took a surprising turn.

What we have to understand is the depth of the problem we had. To say that we could get out of it simply by changing our behavior ignores how deep the problem really is. Only God could help us. He was not giving up; this was the only way out.

In his letters, Paul spends half his time talking about the amazing work Jesus did in giving us this grace. But the other half of his time he talks about how we are then to live. The two halves are intimately connected.

What Jesus has brought us actually has a phenomenal effect on the way we live as God's people. This happens in several ways, all working in concert.

First, the righteousness God has placed within us will shine outward. Granted, it may be a process and take time, but when we receive what God has done, we actually become a new creation (2 Corinthians 5:17). The Creator of life puts life within us (Romans 8:10–11) and we will ever-increasingly reflect the new creation that we really are.

Second, we have a new weapon at our disposal in this war to be good—grace. Paul says grace gives us the power to change, whereas the law was powerless in this regard (Romans 8:3). In Luke 18–19 there are two remarkable stories: that of the rich, young ruler, who was attempting to earn God's favor by what he did, and that of Zacchaeus, who failed in what he did but received grace by Jesus simply choosing him. Jesus gave the rich young ruler one more thing he could try to do, at which point the young man gave up. However, by God's grace, we see Zacchaeus changed and freely doing the very thing Jesus asked the young ruler to do. Grace empowers us.

Third, in Jesus we have an example of sacrificial, never-failing love. If God so loved us, that is how we are to love one another (1 John 4:7–11). This, then, is a model of how we are to live and to love our spouses (Ephesians 5:21–33), children, parents (Ephesians 6:1–4) and one another (Romans 12:9–16).

Fourth, God has made a relationship with us so close and personal that we *want* to do good things. We find ourselves acting like a person deeply in love, where even a sacrifice for the one we love seems as if it is a pleasure and privilege. His allure transcends anything the world has to offer, making sin's bondage unpalatable compared to the freedom and goodness of his Kingdom.

Finally, we have God himself living in us (Romans 8:9–11). This is huge. God wants to live his life through us, and he will do it well. Whereas grace is like a student taking a test and getting help from the teacher whenever he asks, this is like the teacher living within us and the two of us taking the test together. In fact, that teacher wants to take the lead, so our role is to let him do so and then see what he does with our lives.

God's Heart for the Nations

One of the keys to living as God's people is to have in our hearts the things that are stirring in God's heart. One such stirring is his heart for the nations. As mentioned in the last chapter, this was one of the sub-themes of the Old Testament. In the New Testament, it blossoms into a major theme.

John 12:20–36 takes place toward the end of Jesus' ministry. It begins with some Greeks (foreigners) who wished to see Jesus. Jesus' odd response was to jump into a profound discourse about the meaning of his upcoming death, to which God even added his own words spoken from heaven. It was as if these people from the nations triggered something deep within him—the love for the world that was driving him to lay down his life. Indeed he says, "But I, when I am lifted up from the earth, will draw all men to myself" (John 12:32).

After he rose from the dead, many of Jesus' last words concerned his sending us into the world. The Great Commission told us to "make disciples of all nations" (Matthew 28:19). Just before he ascended into heaven, he spoke of the Holy Spirit that would empower us to be witnesses in Jerusalem and "to the ends of the earth" (Acts 1:8). The New Testament shows this theme in blossom. Paul's ministry was devoted to this end, and his letters are written to churches throughout the nations. The book of Acts displays how empowered disciples took the ministry all over the world. It ends with Paul imprisoned in Rome, the center of the major civilization of that day.

In light of this one might ask, does God continue to consider Israel special with a unique call? Absolutely. (See Romans 11.) And does he consider the nations special with calls of their own? Absolutely. It is silly to think that when God considers one nation special he ceases to think another one is special. The same is true of people. In our own families, we consider each of our children special and delight in who they are, loving each with all our hearts. So it is with God. His heart for both Israel and the nations is fascinating and wonderful.

III. KNOWING GOD

The New Testament shows how the search for the Messiah became surprisingly fulfilled and how the quest to live as God's people took an unexpectedly wonderful turn. Knowing God is another theme that was fulfilled in surprising ways.

When Jesus died to give us righteousness, he gave us access to God. Yes, sin and God still do not mix, but when God looks to those who have received Jesus' gift on the cross, he sees Jesus' righteousness. It is described as a robe of righteousness, which we now wear. We have willingly torn away our sinful rags and anything else we were wearing that intruded upon our transparency with God. And in their place, he has given us a beautiful robe. We may not see it physically now, but one day we will look down and see it in amazement when we pass from this world to the next. Even now it is upon us, giving us access to God, who so anxiously awaited our running into his arms. The thought of this reunion was, in fact, his joy as he endured the pain of the cross.

Through Jesus, barriers to knowing God came tumbling down. Matthew 27:51 states that at the very moment Jesus died, the heavy curtain in the temple that separated people from the Holy of Holies was torn in two, symbolizing that the way to Holy God was now open to us. It was as if God ripped it open, like our opening a present at Christmas, in anticipation of what his heart had desired for a long, long time.

John 14

In the New Testament, the theme of knowing God takes on a new aspect that simply boggles my mind. Recently, as I was reading my way through the book of John, I came across chapter 14 and saw it in a way that put this new aspect in a remarkable light.

John 14 begins with Jesus' interaction with Thomas. Jesus had just finished telling the disciples that they will know the way to the place where he is going. Thomas objects,

> *"Lord, we don't know where you are going, so how can we know the way?" Jesus answered, "I am the way and the truth and the life. No one comes to the Father except through me. If you really knew me, you would know my Father as well. From now on, you do know him and have seen him."* (John 14:5–7)

So a discussion of knowing God begins. Philip responds, "Lord, show us the Father and that will be enough" (v. 8). Just seeing God (something that made Moses glow with God's glory for days) may have been enough for Thomas, but Jesus had far more to bring us than that.

This next section of John 14 gives us perhaps the most detailed look into the inner working of the persons of the Trinity in all Scripture. It is such a holy place I call it the "Holy of Holies" of the Bible. Some verses:

- *Don't you believe that I am in the Father, and that the Father is in me? The words I say to you are not just my own. Rather, it is the Father, living in me, who is doing his work. Believe me when I say that I am in the Father and the Father is in me.* (John 14:10–11a)

- *And I will ask the Father, and he will give you another Counselor to be with you forever—the Spirit of truth. The world cannot accept him, because it neither sees him nor knows him.* (John 14:16–17)

- *On that day you will realize that I am in my Father, . . .* (John 14:20)

- *But the Counselor, the Holy Spirit, whom the Father will send in my name, will teach you all things and will remind you of everything I have said to you.* (John 14:26)

- *If you loved me, you would be glad that I am going to the Father, for the Father is greater than I.* (John 14:28b)

In these verses, Jesus describes how intimately the Trinity dwells with one another. Jesus is in the Father and the Father in him. The Holy Spirit is with the Father, the One whom the Father will send.

The persons of the Trinity honor and defer to one another. Jesus honors the Father: "The Father is greater than I" (John 14:28). And in another place the Father honors the Son: "This is my Son, whom I love; with you I am well pleased" (Luke 3:22). Jesus honors the Holy Spirit, calling him the "Spirit of Truth," and the Holy Spirit honors Jesus, reminding us of everything Jesus has said.

If you look at this amazing section of Scripture describing the intimacy of the godhead, you will see I left out some verses. As I was reading it a while ago, my eyes first fell on the verses above as I contemplated the wonder of the Trinity. But then it was as if God highlighted these other verses, interspersed among the ones above:

- *But you know him [the Spirit], for he lives with you and will be in you.* (John 14:17b)

- *You are in me, and I am in you.* (John 14:20b)

- *My Father will love him, and we will come to him and make our home with him.* (John 14:23b)

Suddenly, we find *ourselves* interspersed in these verses. This goes way beyond our original concept of knowing God. We find ourselves in this intimate interaction within the Trinity! First in verse 17, the Spirit lives with us and will be in us. Then in verse 20, Jesus is in us and we in him. Then in verse 23, Jesus and the Father will love us, come to us and make their home in us. This is not just in heaven after we die, though it will be there, too. Jesus was talking in the context of

> The intimacy within the Trinity is astounding enough, but to find ourselves placed in their midst is almost too much to comprehend.

what would happen soon, when he went to the Father (v. 12). The intimacy within the Trinity is astounding enough, but to find ourselves placed in their midst is almost too much to comprehend.

John 14 takes us into yet another aspect of knowing God. There are some more verses in this section of Scripture which I left out. In my own youth, I remember some of the best bonding with my own father was when I went to work with him. God knows that, too, and would have us partner with him in his work:

- *Or at least believe on the evidence of the miracles* [works] *themselves.* (John 14:11b)

- *I tell you the truth, anyone who has faith in me will do what I have been doing. He will do even greater things than these, because I am going to the Father. And I will do whatever you ask in my name, so that the Son may bring glory to the Father. You may ask me for anything in my name, and I will do it.* (John 14:12–14)

If the church could even partially understand the concept of God's desire to partner with us, it would be transformed. He is at work, and we get to be a part of it. The works in these verses, which he invites us to partner in, actually refer to miracles, but they could include anything we do. In some situations, inviting someone over to dinner may be the greater work. Then, at dinner, we might get a chance to pray for their healing, and at that time healing may be the greater work. Like Jesus, who only did what he saw the Father doing (John 5:19), we get to see and partner with God in what he does. Each time I see this happen in my life I am left speechless by the mercy, love, and power of our God whose works I get to experience close-up. Partnering with him in these works is like finding the treasure in the field—being willing to sell all just to enjoy his partnership more and more. But being able to be in the midst of our amazing God—the Father, Son, and Holy Spirit—is what is the greatest treasure of all.

I must say, too, that seeing the Godhead honor and defer to one another in this section is an example to us to honor and defer to one another in the body of Christ. This we have an opportunity to do as we partner with one another in loving him and furthering his remarkable cause. This truly is the way he wants us to live as God's people, and it must put a smile on his face when he sees us do it. And as the world sees how we love one another, then they will indeed know that God has sent the Son (John 17:21).

The Messiah has come! And we get to know him, the Father, and the Holy Spirit in astounding ways.

Thinking More About It

Ω Read some of the New Testament putting yourself in the shoes of Jesus as you speak the words he spoke. Read some of the dialogue out loud, trying to express his heart and inflect the words in the way he might have spoken them.

Ω What were the things that Jesus was passionate about telling us—things that he strongly felt we should know?

CHAPTER FOUR

THE BOOKS OF THE OLD TESTAMENT

The books of the Old Testament are ordered so that they fall into three major categories:

    I. **Historical**: Genesis to Esther (17 books)

    II. **Poetic**: Job to Song of Songs (5 books)

    III. **Prophetic**: Isaiah to Malachi (17 books)

This chapter gives a listing of the books plus a very brief description of each. It would be useful for your future endeavors to commit this information to memory—not word for word, but enough so that, if given a description, you would be able to name the book, or, if given name of the book, you would be able to give a description. Then if you ever need to quickly turn to the ministry of Elijah, for example, you will know to turn to 1 Kings or 2 Chronicles.

    The three major categories above are also broken into sub-categories, as shown throughout this chapter. Therefore you will see that there is a definite order to the way the books were placed in the Old Testament.

I. THE HISTORICAL BOOKS

The historical books trace the rise, fall, and restoration of Israel, a people whom God had chosen to come to know him and to live as he desired . . . and out of whom would come the Messiah who would save them from their failure to do so.

The Pentateuch

These are the first five books of the Bible (also called the *Torah* and sometimes referred to as the Law) written by Moses.

Genesis: (*"beginnings"*) The creation of the world and of man, the fall of man, the flood, the lives of Abraham, Isaac, Jacob, and Joseph.

Exodus: (*the escape from Egypt*) The birth and life of Moses, the plagues on Egypt, the Exodus, and the receiving of the Ten Commandments.

Leviticus: (*"pertaining to the Levites"*) The priestly duties of the Levites—offerings, cleanliness, feasts, rules of conduct.

Numbers: (*named after two censuses taken*) The rebellions of Israel and the subsequent wanderings in the desert for forty years.

Deuteronomy: (*"second law"*) Summary of the wanderings in the desert and a restatement of the laws and how to live as God's nation. It ends with Moses' death.

Israel prior to its Kings

Moses led the people toward the Promised Land but died before entering it. It was Joshua who finally brought Israel into that land. These books are about the history of Israel up to the time of Israel's kings.

Joshua: (*Moses' successor*) Crossing the Jordan to take over Canaan—the future home of Israel—and conquering the land, city by city.

Judges: (*the three hundred years when various judges ruled Israel*) The various judges in Israel: Deborah, Gideon, Samson, etc.

Ruth: (*the great-grandmother of David*) The story of Ruth, a Moabite, who was wonderfully dedicated to God, Israel, her mother-in-law, Naomi, and her husband, Boaz.

Israel under its Kings

Although God was against the idea, the people of Israel clamored for a king, which God gave to them. These are the accounts of those kings and the prophets who ministered during that time.

1 Samuel: (*Samuel and Saul*) The life of Samuel (God's prophet to anoint the kings), the reign of King Saul, the early adventures of David.

2 Samuel: (*David*) The reign of King David.

1 Kings: (*Solomon and Elijah*) The life of King Solomon (David's son), the split of Israel into Judah (the southern kingdom containing Jerusalem, comprised of the tribes of Judah and Benjamin) and Israel (the northern kingdom, comprised of the other ten tribes), the prophet Elijah, and the early kings of Judah and Israel.

2 Kings: (*Elisha and the falls of Israel and Judah*) The life of the prophet Elisha (Elijah's successor), various kings of Judah and Israel, and the fall of Israel and then of Judah.

1 Chronicles: (*parallels 2 Samuel*)

2 Chronicles: (*parallels 1 and 2 Kings*)

Israel after its Fall and Exile

First Israel fell, then Judah, whose people were in exile in Babylon for seventy years. After this some were allowed to return to Jerusalem to rebuild the city.

Ezra: (*the return from exile*) How Cyrus let the Jews return to their land, the rebuilding of the Temple, the perspective of Ezra the priest.

Nehemiah: (*rebuilding the wall*) Nehemiah's burden for Jerusalem and how he oversaw the rebuilding of the wall amid much hardship.

Esther: *(a Jewish queen of Persia)* Esther's courageous defense of the Jewish people as she broke apart a scheme for their destruction.

II. THE POETIC BOOKS

These books are not accounts of Israel's history, but rather songs, wisdom, and lessons to be learned.

Job: (*faith in the face of suffering*) Perhaps the earliest-written book of the Bible, Job tells why and why not the righteous sometimes suffer.

Psalms: (*a songbook*) Written mostly by David, but also by Asaph, Solomon, Moses, and the sons of Korah. These are songs of trust, praise, rejoicing, and mercy.

Proverbs: (*wise sayings*) Written mostly by Solomon, Proverbs is a storehouse of sayings about wisdom, righteousness, the fear of God, and right and wrong.

Ecclesiastes: (*wisdom about earthly life*) Written by Solomon, Ecclesiastes tells us the world only has vanity to offer, so we should fear God.

Song of Songs: (*the beauty of wedded love*) Written by Solomon, this is about a wife's love for the king and his love for her, using intimate, romantic imagery.

III. THE PROPHETIC BOOKS

To understand the prophetic books, here is a brief review of the chronology of Israel and Judah:

- 933 BC — Judah and Israel become divided kingdoms
- 721 BC — Israel (and Samaria, its capital) falls
- 606 BC — Many in Judah are exiled to Babylon
- 586 BC — Judah (and Jerusalem, its capital) falls
- 536 BC — The return from captivity in Babylon

The contents of the prophetic books fall into three general topics:

- A. Warnings to Israel or Judah
- B. Warnings to Other Nations
- C. Coming Hope

Therefore the prophetic books are words of both forth-telling and fore-telling. Even though the warnings were to the people of that time, God intends the people of our day to listen. In addition to the "two mountain peaks" spoken of earlier (the first and second comings of the Messiah), the prophets often saw a third peak—the coming release of their people from captivity—when they prophesied of the coming hope, sometimes bouncing from "peak to peak" in their writings. Often passages have multiple applications in this regard. (See, for example, Isaiah 51:11.)

The books in this section are divided into two categories: the Major Prophets (so named because these books are longer) and the twelve Minor Prophets.

The Major Prophets

Isaiah: (*prophet in Judah around the time when Israel fell*) Warns Judah of its sin, predicts its fall, predicts the fall of Babylon, tells of the wonderful things in store for God's people after the Exile. It contains many astounding predictions about the Messiah.

Jeremiah: (*prophet in Judah during its fall*) Tells Judah of its sin and impending calamity, predicts a seventy-year exile, describes the actual fall of Jerusalem.

Lamentations: (*Jeremiah laments over Jerusalem's fall*) Jeremiah grieves over Jerusalem and prays for mercy.

Ezekiel: (*prophet in Babylon during fall of Jerusalem*) In the Spirit, Ezekiel sees Jerusalem's sins and its fall. He also sees a vision of Israel (the dry bones) coming back to life.

Daniel: (*prophet in Babylon during the Exile and return*) Daniel's remarkable prophetic activities during the Exile. Usually through dreams, he predicts world history: the fall of Babylon and beyond, the coming of the Messiah, the end times.

The Minor Prophets

Hosea: (*prophet in Israel before and during its fall*) Hosea married a prostitute to show the Israelites how they looked to God. Speaks of God's anger and love, and the punishment and restoration of Israel.

Joel: (*prophet in early Judah*) Speaks of a locust plague (coming invasion of Judah or end times?), repentance, a great outpouring of the Spirit, judgment, and harvest.

Amos: (*prophet in Judah prophesying to Israel before its fall*) Warns Israel of destruction because of their sin.

Obadiah: (*prophet in Judah at a time when it was plundered*) Prophesies against Edom, who aided Babylon in plundering Judah. Edom will be wiped out; the Jewish people will return.

Jonah: (*prophet in Israel long before its fall*) Jonah is to tell Nineveh to repent. Jonah's early refusal leads to an episode inside a fish. Hearing Jonah, Nineveh repents.

Micah: (*prophet in Judah before and during Israel's fall*) Woes to Samaria and Jerusalem who are about to fall. God will again rule from Zion. The Messiah is to come out of Bethlehem.

Nahum: (*prophet in Israel one hundred years after its fall*) Says that Nineveh will be destroyed.

Habakkuk: (*prophet in Judah just before its fall*) Questions how God can let Judah fall to a people more wicked than they are. Prediction of Babylon's destruction.

Zephaniah: (*prophet in Judah just before its exile*) To Judah and the nations: the day of judgment is coming. But through it God's people, a humble remnant, will return with joy.

Haggai: (*prophet in Jerusalem after the Exile*) Says to resume work on the Temple—the crops won't suffer. Speaks of the future glory of the Temple.

Zechariah: (*prophet in Jerusalem after the Exile*) Warns not to sin again. Says the Lord himself is the wall to their city. Speaks of the Good Shepherd to come.

Malachi: (*prophet in Jerusalem one hundred years after the Exile*) Warns against corrupt sacrifices (sick animals, etc.). Says the Lord's Day is coming, but Elijah will be sent first.

Thinking More About It

Ω Have a friend quiz you on the books and their basic contents.

Ω Take the quiz on the Old Testament books in the appendix of this book.

CHAPTER FIVE

THE BOOKS OF THE NEW TESTAMENT

The books of the New Testament are divided into three major categories, much like the structure of the Old Testament:

    I. Historical: Matthew to Acts (5 books)

   II. Letters: Romans to Jude (21 books)

  III. Prophetic: Revelation (1 book)

These three major categories are broken into subcategories, as was true in the last chapter. However, since the span of time is not nearly as long as that of the Old Testament, the number of subcategories is less.

I. THE HISTORICAL BOOKS

The historical books (which, of course, do much more than state history) trace the life of Jesus and, in Acts, the life of the disciples and the early church after Jesus ascended into heaven.

The Synoptic Gospels

The first three books of the New Testament, describing the life, ministry, death, and resurrection of Jesus, are so similar they are called "synoptic," meaning "through one eye." Some have tried to explain this similarity by postulating they used a common source (which they call "J"). My own thought is that Matthew and Mark (or Peter, who used Mark as his interpreter) ministered together a lot, which explains their similarity. Luke, in turn, interviewed these men and their acquaintances as he sought to do as much research as he could before writing his book. This is just a guess, and it does not really matter how they came to be so similar. What is fascinating is how they differ in perspective, emphases, and style, each contributing to our picture of the King of all kings.

Matthew: (*written by the Matthew who was most likely the ex-tax-collector disciple of Jesus*) This gospel is very Jewish, having many Old Testament links: prophecies fulfilled, an expansion of the Law (the Sermon on the Mount), a clear call to repentance, the importance of forgiveness.

Mark: (*written by the Mark who was most likely Barnabas's cousin; he was thought to have interpreted for Peter*) This gospel is very action oriented, perhaps being a written version of the gospel proclaimed by Peter. In it we are placed in the action of Jesus and the Kingdom of God invading the world bound by the enemy. It often shows the crowds amazed, leaving us amazed and full of expectant faith.

Luke: (*written by Dr. Luke, Paul's companion*) This gospel emphasizes how Jesus is for everyone (its genealogy goes back to Adam) and has a strong emphasis on the Holy Spirit and the actions of empowered disciples. It was carefully researched and presented in an orderly way (Luke 1:1–4) and contains many beautiful narratives (the Christmas story, the prodigal son, etc.).

The Gospel of John

John: (*written by the disciple John*) Written later than the synoptic Gospels, John probably intended to not repeat many stories told in Matthew, Mark, and Luke, but to tell other incidents and teachings. It centers on Jesus: God who became flesh and our sacrificial Lamb. Though the language is very simple, it is a profoundly deep look at the greatness of Jesus through Spirit-filled eyes.

The Acts of the Apostles

Acts: (*a continuation of Luke's Gospel*) This book is a continuation of the works of Jesus through the church as it encountered all types and conditions of men. It is the Holy Spirit in action—the Word going out into all the world and conquering it. In one sense, we are continuing to "write" the book of Acts today!

II. THE LETTERS

The Letters (or Epistles) were written by Paul, James, Peter, John, and Jude.

The Epistles of Paul

To put Paul's letters into their proper context, know that Paul took three missionary journeys. During these he wrote to the churches that he had previously visited (or founded) or that he intended to visit in the future. After his three journeys, he was imprisoned in Rome. He was either put to death during this imprisonment or, perhaps more likely, was let go, imprisoned again, and then put to death.

Romans: (*written by Paul on his third missionary journey, at Corinth*) Paul, planning a new missionary journey with Rome as its hub, sends a letter showing where he stands. It builds a remarkable foundation of our salvation by grace through faith in Christ.

1 Corinthians: (*written by Paul on his third missionary journey, at Ephesus*) Paul writes to a church with problems: divisions, supposed freedom to sin, disorderly worship services, no true love.

2 Corinthians: (*written by Paul on his third missionary journey, perhaps still at Ephesus*) Paul writes another letter so that reconciliation might be complete.

Galatians: (*written by Paul, perhaps on his first missionary journey*) This was written to counteract the Judaizers, who tried to put Christians back under the Law. As in Romans, Paul establishes that salvation comes by grace, not through the Law.

Ephesians: (*written by Paul imprisoned in Rome*) Paul, to strengthen young churches, holds up the greatness of the church—its position in the heavenly realms, its task and authority.

Philippians: (*written by Paul imprisoned in Rome*) Paul writes a letter to a generous people. This letter is full of "jewels" and encouragement.

Colossians: (*written by Paul imprisoned in Rome*) Paul, perhaps responding to some who said "elemental spirits" were mediators between God and man, lifts up Jesus and shows he is God and the only mediator between God and man.

1 Thessalonians: (*written by Paul on his second missionary journey, at Corinth*) Paul writes to a church doing fine, except for some problems remaining pure in a Gentile environment. To strengthen their hopes, Paul writes a remarkable account of Jesus' second coming.

2 Thessalonians: (*written by Paul on his second missionary journey, at Corinth*) The Thessalonians had overreacted to the message of the Second Coming—some of them had quit their jobs.

1 Timothy: (*written by Paul after his release from prison in Rome*) Paul writes to a young pastor, Timothy, how to handle problems in the church.

2 Timothy: (*written by Paul, imprisoned just before his death?*) Paul tells Timothy some things he wants him to hear before his (Paul's) execution.

Titus: (*written by Paul about the time he wrote 1 Timothy*) Paul tells Titus much of what he said in 1 Timothy.

Philemon: (*written by Paul during his first imprisonment in Rome*) Paul pleads for Onesimus, Philemon's runaway slave, now a Christian.

The Other Epistles

Hebrews: (*the author of this epistle is unknown—perhaps Paul or Barnabas*) Written to Jewish Christians whose faith once was strong, but now weakened. The letter points to Jesus as the glorious fulfillment and full reality of all that is in the Old Testament.

James: (*written by James, head of the Jerusalem church, perhaps Jesus' brother*) A practical Word: practice must follow profession. The power of prayer.

1 Peter: (*written by the disciple Peter in Rome*) This is a letter of hope to persecuted Christians. We are a royal priesthood, strangers in the world. Live in love.

2 Peter: (*written by Peter*) What to watch out for while living in these evil last times.

1 John: (*written by the disciple John*) John writes in response to Gnosticism: a heresy saying Jesus was never really in the flesh. John describes the Lord and what our reactions to him must be: don't sin, be forgiven, love one another.

2 John: (*written by John*) John writes to a church: love one another and watch for deceivers.

3 John: (*written by John*) John writes to a friend about a "leader" who is against John's missionaries.

Jude: (*written by Jude, the brother of James*) Jude writes against men who thought it was all right to sin.

III. THE PROPHETIC BOOK

This contains Jesus' letters to the churches and a prophetic depiction of what is to come.

Revelation: (*written by John, in exile on the island of Patmos*) Revelation is a comfort to those undergoing persecution. It shows how God is in control and everything will turn out as he planned it. There is much symbolism. (For example, 3=God, 6=man, 7=perfection, 666=man acting as God). There are seven major visions: 1) letters to the seven churches; 2) seven seals; 3) seven trumpets; 4) a woman and two beasts; 5) seven plagues; 6) the overthrow of God's enemies; 7) a new heaven and earth. (It's nice to flip to the "last page of the book" and see how everything is going to turn out!)

Thinking More About It

Ω Have a friend quiz you on the books and their basic contents.

Ω Take the quiz on the New Testament books in the appendix of this book.

CHAPTER SIX

GREEK: THE LANGUAGE OF THE NEW TESTAMENT

I'm starting with the language of the New Testament rather than the Old mainly because Greek is a much easier language to understand. It has an alphabet somewhat similar to English (though its characters are different) and, like English, it reads from left to right. There are also many English words that come from the Greek, so some Greek words will be familiar to us.

There were actually two forms of Greek being used in the days of the New Testament: classical Greek, the language of Greek literature, and Koine (meaning *common*) Greek, the language of the common man. In that day a movement of purists, called Atticists, regarded classical Greek as the only acceptable standard for writing prose. It is interesting that the New Testament was written in Koine Greek. It had no pretenses—it was written in the language of common people in order to touch the hearts of common people.

In New Testament Israel, Greek was a second language to many of the people. Aramaic was the language Jesus and the disciples would have spoken day by day. However, when the Good News of Jesus went out into the world, Greek would have been the natural choice and was most likely the language used when most of the New Testament was penned.

The Greek Alphabet

Upper	Lower	Name	English
Α	α	alpha	a (short)
Β	β	beta	b
Γ	γ	gamma	g (hard)
Δ	δ	delta	d
Ε	ε	epsilon	e (short)
Ζ	ζ	zeta	z
Η	η	eta	e (long a)
Θ	θ	theta	th
Ι	ι	iota	i (long e)
Κ	κ	kappa	k
Λ	λ	lambda	l
Μ	μ	mu	m
Ν	ν	nu	n
Ξ	ξ	xi	x
Ο	ο	omicron	o (short)
Π	π	pi	p
Ρ	ρ	rho	r
Σ	σ, ς	sigma	s
Τ	τ	tau	t
Υ	υ	upsilon	u (long)
Φ	φ	phi	ph
Χ	χ	chi	ch (soft k)
Ψ	ψ	psi	ps
Ω	ω	omega	o (long)

CHAPTER 6

THE GREEK LANGUAGE

It is my intent to just present enough of the Greek and Hebrew languages to be useful and interesting to most people. That is not to say studying these languages in depth is not useful and interesting, but both languages can become very complicated with all of their special forms, rules, and exceptions to the rules (in the same way English can be complicated for someone learning that language). However, the small introduction I will give should open up a lot of potential for digging into the Scriptures—enough for being able to pronounce Greek words, identify them in interlinear Bibles, and look them up in Greek lexicons. Granted, most of what we learn from the Bible can be obtained through the English translations. But I will give examples of how we can use the Greek and Hebrew for additional insights—the sort of gems that you hear from your pastor when he refers to the meaning of words in their original languages.

The Greek Alphabet

The Greek alphabet is shown on the previous page. Notice that, like English, each letter has an upper and lower case. One letter, sigma, has two versions of its lower case. The latter (ς) is used only when it is the final letter of a word.

When a word begins with a vowel, one of two marks is placed over it: ἀ or ἁ. The first is a smooth breathing mark and does not change the pronunciation. The latter is a rough breathing mark and gives it an "h" sound. Greek also contains accent marks: a small slash or semicircle above a portion of a word (such as θεὸς , λόγος, or φῶς).

There are a few cases where combinations of letters produce different sounds. (English has many of these: "sh," "th," and "ng," for example.) In Greek, the only consonant that works this way is when γ (gamma) is in one of these combinations: γγ, γκ, or γχ, in which case the g has an "ng" sound. (For example, ἄγγελος is pronounced "angelos" which means "angel.")

Likewise, several vowels can be combined to produce new vowel sounds:

αι   pronounced like the *ai* in *aisle*
αυ   pronounced like the *ow* in *now*
ει   pronounced like the *ei* in *reign*
ευ   pronounced like the *e* in *bet* or *oo* in *moon*
οι   pronounced like the *oy* in *boy*
ου   pronounced like the *oo* in *moon*
υι   pronounced like the word *we*

Like English, capital letters are used at the beginning of names. Unlike English, they are only used at the beginning of sentences if the sentence starts a paragraph or quotation. Periods and commas are the same as in English. However, in Greek a question mark looks like a semicolon, and a colon or semicolon looks like a raised period.

Advantages of Looking at the Greek Text

As I said before, most of what you learn from Scripture you can obtain with an English translation. However, there are some advantages in looking at the Greek text.

Greek words can have different nuances than their English counterparts. For example, the word for "hope" (*elpis*) (as is used in Hebrews 11:1, "Faith is being sure of what we hope for.") means "confident expectation" in Greek. Although this may have also been the connotation in English at one time, now hope has a little more doubt associated with it: the feeling that what is desired is also possible. Going to the Greek brings us to the correct interpretation. (Greek words may also have multiple meanings that are different from their English counterparts.)

English words may have several Greek counterparts. For words where this is true, it is often instructive to ponder the reason why one word was chosen over another. For example, there are two words for "love" used in the Bible: *agapao* and *phileo*. *Agapao* is the never-failing love God has toward us, whereas *phileo* is a tender affection. In the discourse between Jesus and Peter in John 21, both of these are used. When Jesus asks, "Do you love me?" the first two times he uses *agapao*. Peter responds using *phileo*. Having just denied the Lord, Peter knows all too well his love can fail. The third time Jesus uses *phileo*, receiving what Peter can offer. God will receive our love. And though our love can be flawed and fail, God's love certainly cannot, and that provides the foundation for our life in him.

Greek nouns and adjectives change depending on their numbers and cases. Nouns, adjectives, articles (such as "the"), and pronouns all have different forms depending on whether they are singular or plural. For nouns and pronouns, this is similar to English except for the word "you." In Greek you can tell whether "you" refers to one person or many. For example, in John 3:7 where Jesus says, "You must be born again," he uses the plural form of "you." This indicates he was referring to more than just Nicodemus (not a huge revelation, but interesting).

Nouns, adjectives, articles, and pronouns also carry three different grammatical genders (masculine, feminine, and neuter) and have four different cases: nominative (used for the subject of verbs, such as "Bob" in "Bob gave me his pen"), accusative (used for direct objects, "pen" in the example above), dative (used for indirect objects, "me" in the example above), and genitive (used for possession, "his" in the example above). The accusative, dative, and genitive cases are also used for nouns when they are the objects of prepositions.

Since the definite article "the" can have three genders, four cases, and be singular or plural, that means there are twenty-four forms for the word "the" in Greek! The same is true for adjectives and pronouns. And each noun already has a gender, so it can take on eight forms. This may be more than you wanted to know, but you need to be forewarned that if you find a Greek word in the Bible and try looking it up in a Greek dictionary, it may be in one form in the Bible (say dative plural) but is always nominative singular in the dictionary. Fortunately, the forms of most nouns and adjectives are similar enough to one another (they usually differ in their endings) so that you should easily find the word when you look it up, but don't always expect an exact match. The same thing applies to verbs, as I will discuss below.

Greek sentences are written so that the articles and adjectives match the cases of the nouns to which they refer. That means that if you were to scramble the words in a Greek sentence, you could still figure out which adjectives are attached to which nouns. For example, in: "The brown cat ate the grey mouse," it would not matter if you changed the word order because "brown" and "cat" would have the same case—the same for "grey" and "mouse." Writers of Greek sometimes took advantage of this freedom and changed the word order in order to highlight certain words. I enjoy looking at an interlinear Bible (where the English is written under the Greek) so I can see the order of the words in a given verse.

Greek verbs have more tenses than in English. The tenses of a verb (such as past, present, and future) have additions in Greek that can sometimes give us more information than the English translation. The past can take an imperfect tense, indicating continuous action, or an aorist tense, indicating one-time action. For instance, "I jumped when I was a child," in the aorist tense, would mean I jumped once. The imperfect would indicate that I jumped repeatedly. The imperative mood has this distinction as well. In Ephesians 5:18 Paul says, "Be filled with the Spirit." Is it a one-time filling? The verb tense indicates he is telling us to continually be filled, something we miss in the English version.

The forms of Greek verbs change according to their tense (such as past or present), mood (such as imperative), person (first, second, third), number (singular or plural), and voice (active, passive, middle). Usually it is the ending that changes. However, the past tense adds an epsilon to the beginning of a verb (or changes its starting vowel). As in English, these different forms often simply add letters to the verb ("talk" and "talked"). Other times they slightly change the verb ("write" and "wrote"). Still other times they greatly change the verb ("is" and "was"). Dictionaries, including the Greek, are usually merciful enough so that if we look up "was" it will inform us it is the past tense of "is" and have us turn there. (Chapter 9 will discuss even easier ways to look up Greek words.)

SAMPLE TRANSLATIONS OF WORDS

It will be very beneficial to learn how to sound out some Greek words. I have chosen some you will probably recognize due to their similarity to words in English. To do this, begin by replacing each Greek letter with its English counterpart using the Greek alphabet in the beginning of this chapter. Then try to guess what it is by its similarity to a word in English. For example:

$$\ἄνθροπος \rightarrow \text{anthropos}$$

That word means "man," similar to "anthropology," which is the study of man. To give you more practice at this, I have ten words you can try translating in Quiz 3 found in the appendix of this book.

EARLY AND MODERN GREEK TEXT

We do not have the original manuscripts of the New or Old Testaments. The earliest piece of the New Testament we have dates in the early second century. We have many pieces (and complete Bibles) later than that. In fact, of all the ancient literature, the Bible is, by far, the best established by its early copies. All together there are many hundreds of differences in the copies, but based on the size of the New Testament and the large number of copies, these are relatively few. Most are very minor, as in the case of spelling differences. Some additions may have come about when someone added a note to the margin which someone then copied into the text years later. Or a deletion occurred when a legitimate addition was made in a margin and was ignored when copied years later. None of the differences lead to any theological disputes. Overall, an extremely high regard for the Word of God caused the ones who copied it to be painstakingly careful in what they did.

Below is a sample of some early text—Matthew 13:14—from a manuscript dating back to the fourth century (Codex Sinaiticus). Early manuscripts such as this were written all in one case (most looked like our current upper case), and there were no chapter or verse numbers, no punctuation, and often no spaces between the words or sentences! (Chapter and verse numbers were added around AD 1200.) Words frequently started on one line and continued onto the next.

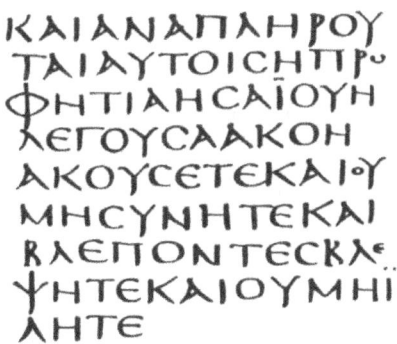

© The British Library Board. All Rights Reserved
3/15/2010. Reprinted with permission.

If we were to do something like this with the English translation, here is how it would look:

> INTHEMISFULFILLEDTHEPROPHEC
> YOFISAIAHYOUWILLBEEVERHEARI
> NGBUTNEVERUNDERSTANDINGYO
> UWILLEVERBESEEINGBUTNEVERP
> ERCEIVING

Here is the same verse, Matthew 13:14, as it is found in current Greek New Testaments:

> 14 καὶ ἀναπληροῦται αὐτοῖς ἡ προφητεία Ἠσαΐου ἡ λέγουσα· Ἀκοῇ ἀκούσετε καὶ οὐ μὴ συνῆτε, καὶ βλέποντες βλέψετε καὶ οὐ μὴ ἴδητε.

Here is the same verse in interlinear format:

> 14 και ʼἀναπληροῦται αὐτοῖς ἡ προφητεία
>   And   is fulfilled   in them the prophecy
> Ἠσαΐου ἡ λέγουσα· Ἀκοῇ ἀκούσετε καὶ οὐ μη
> of Isaiah the one saying: in hearing you will hear and certainly not
> συνῆτε, καὶ βλέποντες βλέψετε καὶ οὐ μὴ ἴδητε.
> understand, and seeing   you will see and certainly not perceive.

Finally, here is the verse in the NIV:

> 14 In them is fulfilled the prophecy of Isaiah: "You will be ever hearing but never understanding; you will ever be seeing but never perceiving."

If nothing else, this makes us appreciate having the Word of God in our own language, giving us a chance to both "see and perceive." May this chance be given in every language.

Thinking More About It

Ω Take the quiz on Greek words in the appendix of this book.

CHAPTER SEVEN

HEBREW: THE LANGUAGE OF THE OLD TESTAMENT

Because it is so different from English, Hebrew tends to be harder to learn than Greek. Yet that makes it fascinating, too. The biggest differences are that it reads from right to left and the letters are unlike anything most people have seen. Also, prior to AD 800, the alphabet only represented the consonants—the pronunciation of the vowels was passed down orally.

THE HEBREW ALPHABET AND VOWEL MARKS

The Hebrew alphabet is shown on the next page. Notice there is only one case—no upper and lower cases like English and Greek. Several of the letters (*kaph, mem, nun, pe,* and *tsadhe*) have second forms that are used as the final letter of words. *Sin* and *shin* have two pronunciations depending on where the dot is placed above them. Six of the letters may or may not have a dot (called a *dagesh*) in their midst which can change their pronunciations. The *dagesh* can also be placed inside other letters, lengthening their sound (changing *mem*, for example, from "m" to "mm"). (The *dagesh* was invented by the Masorites who will be mentioned later.) Two of the letters (*aleph* and *ayin*) have no sound as a consonant; only the added vowel sound is pronounced.

The Hebrew Alphabet

Letter	Name	English
א	aleph	none
ב	beth	b (v w/o dot)
ג	gimel	g (g w/o dot)
ד	daleth	d (d w/o dot)
ה	he	h
ו	waw	w (or v or u)
ז	zayin	z
ח	heth	ch (soft k)
ט	teth	t
י	yodh	y
כ, ך	kaph	k (kh w/o dot)
ל	lamedh	l
מ, ם	mem	m
נ, ן	nun	n
ס	samekh	s
ע	ayin	none
פ, ף	pe	p (ph w/o dot)
צ, ץ	tsadhe	ts
ק	qoph	q
ר	resh	r
שׂ, שׁ	sin, shin	s, sh
ת	taw	t (th w/o dot)

Vowel Marks

Symbol	English
Xָה	a (longer)
Xָ	a (longer)
Xַ	a (short)
Xֲ	a (half)
Xֵי	e (long a)
Xֵ	e (long a)
Xֶ	e (short)
Xֱ	e (half)
Xִי	i (long e)
Xִ	i (short)
Xוֹ	o (long)
Xֹ	o (long)
Xָ	o (shorter)
Xֳ	o (half)
Xוּ	u (long)
Xֻ	u (shorter)
Xְ	silent

CHAPTER 7

The letter *waw* was pronounced as a "w" in ancient times. Later (as is now the case in modern Hebrew) it became pronounced as a "v" (and the letter called *vav*).

In the ninth and tenth centuries AD, the Masorites in Tiberias perfected a system of vowel notation and began adding it to the Hebrew text. This is shown on the right half of the table on the previous page. ("X" represents any Hebrew letter.) In this table "longer" means slightly longer than the short English sound of the vowel, and "shorter" means slightly shorter than the long English sound. "Half" means that the vowel is pronounced for a short amount of time. "Silent" indicates no vowel or an extremely short e sound. Notice that *yodh*, *waw*, and a final *he* are sometimes used to form some long vowel sounds. In all but the earliest Hebrew writing (prior to the tenth century BC), these three letters were written to express these vowels (but without the dots until the Masorites added them).

SAMPLE TRANSLATIONS OF WORDS

Due to the vowel marks, it will be a little harder to sound out the Hebrew words than it was for Greek. Begin by replacing the Hebrew letters with those in English and write the vowels below the letters as shown below. Then put all the letters in order from left to right. For example:

יִשְׂרָאֵל → L'RSY → YISRAEL
            e a   i

This is the word for "Israel." (To give you more practice at this, I have ten more Hebrew words you can try translating in Quiz 4 in the appendix of this book.)

Here is another one for interest. It is "Yahweh," the covenant name of God:

יהוה → H W H Y → Y H W H

Note that there are no vowel marks. That is because this name was so revered that no one would even pronounce it—they would say *Adonai* (meaning Lord) instead. The symbols for Yahweh are often referred to as the *tetragrammaton* (meaning "four letters") and is often written YHVH. In the NIV, the translated word is written as "LORD" (uppercase). In Old English it is written as "Jehovah." (The "J" actually comes from the history of the Romance languages. In the late medieval period, the letter *J* was a variation of the letter *I* and both were pronounced as "i" or "y." Then *J* started taking on its own pronunciation. In Spanish it took on an "h" sound; in French and English it took on its current "j" sound. In Hebrew, however, the beginning *yodh* was always pronounced as a "y.")

HEBREW NOUNS AND VERBS

The Hebrew nouns come in two genders: masculine and feminine. They also come in three numbers: singular, plural, and dual (indicating two of something). These will affect the form of nouns, but unlike Greek, their case in the sentence (nominative, accusative, etc.) will not. Nouns are usually made plural by adding "im" (masculine) or "oth" (feminine) at the end of the noun.

The direct article ("the") is not a separate word in Hebrew. Instead "ha" is added to the beginning of a word (or "et" if the noun is a direct object). So "the Messiah" is written "hamashiach." Possessive pronouns (such as "my" and "his") are written as special endings on the nouns they modify.

The prepositions "in" and "to" are attached to the beginning of Hebrew nouns: using "be" and "le" accordingly. So also is the word "and" where "w" is attached to its beginning.

The verb "is" is often left out. It is only implied.

Hebrew verbs, in their simplest forms, are usually only three letters. But things get more complicated from there. First, verb forms depend on number (singular or plural), person (first, second, third), and gender (masculine or feminine). Second, verb forms depend on tense, such as perfect (used for past or present), imperfect (used for future, customary, or possible action), and imperative. Third, every verb can take on one or more types: *Qal*, *Niphal*, *Piel*, *Pual*, *Hiphel*, *Hophal*, and *Hithpael*. These affect the verb's meaning. So the word for "break" might mean "was broken" in *Niphal*, "smash" in *Piel*, "was smashed" in *Pual*, "cause to break" in *Hiphel*, "was caused to break" in *Hophal*, and "broke itself" in *Hithpael*. (Lexicons will tell you what the various forms mean for each verb.)

Most of these things: the number, person, gender, and tense of a verb usually affect its ending. Furthermore, the verb's type can also add a letter to the beginning of a verb. There are many rules as to how verbs change, and there are many exceptions to the rules! The result (which is why I told you about all this) is that if you pluck a Hebrew verb out of a verse, all these forms can make it a nightmare to try to find the verb in a Hebrew lexicon. The best thing to do is identify the three-letter root of the verb and look it up. Either that or look into my shortcuts in chapter 9.

EARLY AND MODERN HEBREW TEXT

The following is from the Dead Sea Scrolls (the Isaiah scroll) dating from the first century BC. Part of Isaiah 7:14 is near the bottom of this section. Notice that, unlike the ancient Greek manuscript, it does separate words with spaces.

הֲאָבֶר אל אחיו לאמין שאל לו אות מאב .אדוה אן יוה׃
אלי או הגבה למעלה ויאמר אחז לא אשאל ולא
אנ׳ יהוה ויאמר שמעו נא בת דוד המעט מכם
הלאות אנשים כי תלאו גם את אלהי לכן יתן מ׳ הוא
לכם אות הנה העלמה הרה וילדת בן וקראת שמו עמנו אל

Reprinted with permission from The Israel Museum, Jerusalem.

Here is Isaiah 7:14 in a modern Hebrew Bible:

14 לָכֵן יִתֵּן אֲדֹנָי הוּא לָכֶם אוֹת הִנֵּה הָעַלְמָה
הָרָה וְיֹלֶדֶת בֵּן וְקָרָאת שְׁמוֹ עִמָּנוּ אֵל:

Here is the same verse in interlinear format: (Read it from right to left.)

הָעַלְמָה	הִנֵּה	אוֹת	לָכֶם	הוּא	אֲדֹנָי	יִתֵּן	לָכֵן 14
the virgin	behold	a sign	to you	himself	the Lord	will give	Therefore

אֵל:	עִמָּנוּ	שְׁמוֹ	וְקָרָאת	בֵּן	וְיֹלֶדֶת	הָרָה
God	with us	his name	and calls	a son	and bears	conceives

Finally, here is the verse in the NIV:

14 Therefore the Lord himself will give you a sign: The virgin will be with child and will give birth to a son, and will call him Immanuel.

I also wanted to note that, while most of the Old Testament was first written in Hebrew, parts of Daniel and Ezra were originally written in Aramaic, a language similar to Hebrew, used from the second Temple period into Jesus' day.

This concludes our look into the original languages of the Bible. Now onto what the Bible says and how to dig into it, teach it, and use it.

Thinking More About It

Ω Take the quiz on Hebrew words in the appendix of this book.

CHAPTER EIGHT

Systematic Theology

As I said at the beginning of this book, God did not write the Bible to be like a theology book. That does not mean, however, that we should not collect what we learn about God and write it out it an orderly fashion. That is an immense help not only in solidifying our own understanding, but in assuring that everyone in the church has a grasp on the foundational truths of our faith. It also helps us as teachers to make sure that we "major on the majors" and not over-emphasize minor points.

Organizing the truths of Scripture is what is called *systematic theology*. In this chapter I will merely skim through the points, offering some discussion and supplying some pertinent Scriptures. Most systematic theology books are huge, and systematic theologians, such as Wayne Grudem, have made such theology into an art form.

What is important to remember here is that we are organizing thoughts from Scripture, therefore the Bible is the sole source of truth. I would encourage you to be a "Berean" (Acts 17:11) when being presented with what someone says and check it out in Scripture yourself. Remember, too, that when looking at proof texts, often the context and verses from other parts of the Bible come into play when uncovering the overall picture of what a text is trying to say. In chapter 9 we will look at this process in detail. Of course, reading the Bible repeatedly is invaluable in being able to discern the veracity of what you read or hear.

There are a number of ways to organize a system of theology, although most systematic theology texts end up covering many of the same topics. In this chapter I am going to organize the general topics as follows:

　　I. **God**: *His Attributes, The Trinity*

　　II. **The Cross**: *The Nature of Man, Jesus Became Man, The Work of the Cross, Justification*

　　III. **Our Lives on Earth**: *Sanctification, Carrying Our Crosses, The Church*

　　IV. **Our Lives in Heaven**: *Jesus' Resurrection and Ours, Jesus' Second Coming and the End Times, Final Judgment, Embracing Mystery*

　　V. **The Word of God**: *How the Word Was Written, The Integrity of the Word, Baptism and Communion, Law and Grace*

Many of the points I am going to make are essential to the Christian faith. These points are said to be within the "circle of orthodoxy." The points concerning the nature of God and Jesus' work of salvation especially fall within this circle. Denominations may disagree on some less important points (such as the mode of baptism) that are outside this circle but are still considered orthodox. However, disagreeing on the points within this circle (such as Jesus being God) would be considered embracing teachings that are outside the Christian faith. As for the minor points on which we differ, as much as we might like to be free from denominational differences, we are all influenced by our backgrounds to some degree. This can affect how we apply certain verses or how we use our reasoning to make certain conclusions which Scripture may or may not be implying.

Finally, I would like to end the chapter with some theology that often does not make it into systematic textbooks but is important for Christians to grasp as they struggle with the issues of life.

I. GOD

We begin with a look at what God is like. Of course, the best way to appreciate who God is and what is on his heart is by reading Scripture in its entirety. Nevertheless, the following are some of the attributes of God given in Scripture.

His Attributes

- **God is.** *God said to Moses, "I am who I am. This is what you are to say to the Israelites: 'I AM has sent me to you.'"* (Exodus 3:14)

- **God is a spirit.** *God is spirit, and his worshipers must worship in spirit and in truth.* (John 4:24)

- **God is a living, rational being.** *Oh, the depth of the riches of the wisdom and knowledge of God! How unsearchable his judgments, and his paths beyond tracing out! Who has known the mind of the Lord? Or who has been his counselor?* (Romans 11:33–34)

- **God has a will.** *I desire to do your will, O my God; your law is within my heart.* (Psalm 40:8)

  Note: God has chosen to give man free will, so sometimes God's will (or desire) can be resisted (as in Ezekiel 33:11), other times it will be done regardless (as in Isaiah 46:11).

- **God is eternal.** *Before the mountains were born or you brought forth the earth and the world, from everlasting to everlasting you are God.* (Psalm 90:2)

- **God is unchanging.** *I the LORD do not change.* (Malachi 3:6a) [See also James 1:17.]

- **God is infinite and omnipresent (present everywhere).** *"Do not I fill heaven and earth?" declares the LORD.* (Jeremiah 23:24b)

- **God is omnipotent (all-powerful).** *"I am the Alpha and the Omega," says the Lord God, "who is, and who was, and who is to come, the Almighty."* (Revelation 1:8)

- **God is omniscient (all-knowing).** *For God is greater than our hearts, and he knows everything.* (1 John 3:20)

- **God is holy (sinless and altogether unique).** *There is no one holy like the LORD; there is no one besides you; there is no Rock like our God.* (1 Samuel 2:2) *God is light; in him there is no darkness at all.* (1 John 1:5)

- **God is just.** *Your righteousness is like the mighty mountains, your justice like the great deep.* (Psalm 36:6) *Yet he does not leave the guilty unpunished.* (Exodus 34:7)

- **God is right, true and faithful.** *For the word of the LORD is right and true; he is faithful in all he does.* (Psalm 33:4)

- **God is good.** *For the LORD is good and his love endures forever; his faithfulness continues through all generations.* (Psalm 100:5)

- **God is merciful.** *And he passed in front of Moses, proclaiming, "The LORD, the LORD, the compassionate and gracious God, slow to anger, abounding in love and faithfulness, maintaining love to thousands, and forgiving wickedness, rebellion and sin.* (Exodus 34:6–7a)

  This verse also shows how **God has emotions.**

- **God is loving.** *Whoever does not love, does not know God, because God is love.* (1 John 4:8)

- **God is the creator.** *In the beginning, God created the heavens and the earth.* (Genesis 1:1)

  By this we can see God has unfathomable intelligence and a stunning sense of artistry.

The Trinity

Although the word "Trinity" is not itself in the Scriptures, what it represents is well established there. God is one, yet he is in three distinct persons. Each person is truly God (as I will discuss individually below), but they are not three gods—they are one. How this works is incomprehensible to us. Any attempt to find analogies in the natural world falls terribly short and usually ends in an early-church heresy, in which some group came up with a similar erroneous description of God. Some of the early Christian creeds were written to correct these errors. We simply must stick with what Scripture teaches: one God, three persons. Here is a sampling of what Scripture teaches on this subject.

- **God is one.** *Hear, O Israel: The LORD our God, the LORD is one.* (Deuteronomy 6:4)

- **Scripture refers to three persons.** *Therefore go and make disciples of all nations, baptizing them in the name of the Father and of the Son and of the Holy Spirit."* (Matthew 28:19) [See also 2 Corinthians 13:14 and John 14.]

  Note: It is interesting with "New Testament eyes" to go back to the Old Testament and see the three-fold adulation of the angels in Isaiah 6:3, the three-part Aaronic blessing in Numbers 6:24–26, and how God refers to himself in the plural in Genesis 1:26.

CHAPTER 8

- **The Father is God.** *"Father, . . . Now this is eternal life: that they may know you, the only true God."* (John 17:1–3)

- **The Son is God.** *He [Jesus] is the true God and eternal life.* (1 John 5:20b) [See also John 1:1.]

  Note that Jesus is God is also evidenced by Scripture giving him: 1) divine names: *"My Lord and my God!"* (John 20:28); *Lord of glory* (1 Corinthians 2:8); *Jesus answered, "before Abraham was born, I am!"* (John 8:58); 2) divine attributes: *unchanging and eternal* (Hebrews 13:8), *omnipresent* (Matthew 28:20), *omniscient* (John 21:17), *omnipotent* (Matthew 28:18); and 3) divine worship: *"Let all God's angels worship him"* (Hebrews 1:6). Revelation 19:10 says worship is to be given only to God.

  > That Jesus is God is also evidenced by Scripture giving him divine names, divine attributes, and divine worship.

- **The Holy Spirit is God.** *Then Peter said, "Ananias . . . you have lied to the Holy Spirit . . . You have not lied to men but to God."* (Acts 5:3–4)

"Father" is how Jesus lovingly referred to the first person of the Trinity. The Father is our creator who, being a perfect father, is intimately interested in our well being (Matthew 6:26). Jesus described the Father's heart in the parable of the prodigal son—one longing for us to come home (Luke 15:20).

Jesus, being a perfect son of a perfect father, was fiercely dedicated to his Father's will (John 5:19). He was begotten (John 3:16, KJV, Psalm 2:7, KJV) in eternity past (John 1:1–3), taking part in creation. He is truly God in fullness and substance (Colossians 2:9). He represented his Father perfectly to us (Hebrews 1:3). As I will discuss later, he became man (Philippians 2:6–8), took our sins upon himself (2 Corinthians 5:21), died (Luke 23:46), then rose again (1 Corinthians 15:3–6) that we might live (John 14:19). He ascended to heaven (Luke 24:50–51) and will come again (Acts 1:11). Then he will reign forever over his Kingdom which will have no end (Revelation 11:15). We are forever grateful for the price only he could have paid. He is our passion and he is our friend (John 15:15).

In the person of the Holy Spirit we encounter God closely and personally (John 14:17). He, too, took part in creation (Genesis 1:2). He was sent to us from the Father and the Son (John 15:26). He is life giving (2 Corinthians 3:6, Romans 8:11). He helps us know and live like the Son (2 Corinthians 3:3). He lives in us (2 Timothy 1:14), bears fruit in us (Galatians 5:22–23), and does the works of God through us by participating in his gifts (1 Corinthians 12:7–11) and ministry (the entire book of Acts).

God is amazing!

II. THE CROSS: JESUS' WORK FOR MAN

Someone once said that all theology, and therefore all we teach, must be tied to the cross. It is our center.

To understand the cross, we must understand why we need it, what was accomplished on it, and how to receive it.

The Nature of Man

These Scriptures will show that, although man was created in God's image, the fall of man left him badly in need of a savior. ("Man," of course, refers to mankind, male and female.)

- **God created man in his image.** *Then God said, "Let us make man in our image, in our likeness."* (Genesis 1:26)
- **Man fell.** (Genesis 3)

- **The descendants of Adam were like Adam.** *When Adam had lived 130 years, he had a son in his own likeness, in his own image.* (Genesis 5:3)

- **We are fallen even from birth.** *Surely I was sinful at birth, sinful from the time my mother conceived me.* (Psalm 51:5) [See also Romans 7:18 and Isaiah 64:6.]

This left us spiritually blind (1 Corinthians 2:14), spiritually dead (Ephesians 2:1), inclined to evil (Genesis 8:21), and at enmity with God (Romans 8:7, KJV). Romans 6:23 says the wages of our condition was death (both physically and eternally). Yet God, who created us, still loved us. His heart was torn. As we saw before, God is both merciful and just, so sin could not go unpunished: the wages had to be paid.

> The heart of God came up with a plan, inconceivable to us, a plan in which "mercy and truth have met together; righteousness and peace have kissed."

The heart of God came up with a plan, inconceivable to us, a plan in which "mercy and truth have met together; righteousness and peace have kissed" (Psalm 85:10, NKJV). That plan unfolded with Jesus heading toward one of man's most horrible instruments of torture and death: the cross.

Jesus Became Man

Jesus is truly God. When he came to earth, he also became truly man.

- **Jesus was truly man.** *For there is one God, and one mediator between God and men, the man Christ Jesus.* (1 Timothy 2:5)

Though in very nature he was God, Jesus humbled himself and was made in the likeness of man (Philippians 2:6–8). He had flesh like ours (John 1:14), felt what we feel, yet was without sin (Hebrews

4:15). He was born of a virgin and conceived by the Holy Spirit (Luke 1:34–35), therefore being the son of both God and man, coming to us out of God's desire, not man's (John 3:16, 1:11). For him to come like this was itself part of the price he paid for us.

The Work of the Cross

All four Gospels devote a large part of what they say to the suffering and death of Jesus on the cross. I would like to turn our attention on what that meant and what was accomplished on the cross. Scripture has a great deal to say on this.

First, there is what I call the **great exchange** ("redemption" really means "exchange")—Jesus taking what we deserved and we taking what he deserved.

- **Jesus took on our sin and guilt that we might be forgiven and declared righteous.** *God made him who had no sin to be sin for us, so that in him we might become the righteousness of God.* (2 Corinthians 5:21)

- **Jesus took on our punishment of death that we might live forever.** *So also the result of one act of righteousness was justification that brings life for all men.* (Romans 5:18) [See also Romans 6:23.]

- **Jesus took on our separation from God that we might have fellowship with him.** . . . *My God, my God, why have you forsaken me? . . . And when Jesus had cried out again in a loud voice, he gave up his spirit. At that moment the curtain of the temple was torn in two from top to bottom* [signifying the end of the separation between God and the people]. (Matthew 27:46–51)

- **The prophecy of Isaiah.** *But he was pierced for our transgressions, he was crushed for our iniquities; the* *punishment that brought us peace was upon him, and by his wounds we are healed.* (Isaiah 53:5)

There is also the **great atonement**—the Lamb of God paying the price of the world's sin.

- **Jesus died for the sins of the world.** *He is the atoning sacrifice for our sins, and not only for ours but also for the sins of the whole world.* (1 John 2:2) [See also John 1:29, 1 Timothy 2:6, 2 Corinthians 5:19.]

Though Jesus died for the world and offers this gift to all, desiring all to be saved (1 Timothy 2:4), an individual must still receive it by faith or the gift will do him no good.

There is also the **great victory**—Satan's dominion effectively crushed and the life of God released on the earth.

- **Jesus' death was victory over the enemy.** *So that by his death he might destroy him who holds the power of death—that is, the devil.* (Hebrews 2:14) [See also Revelation 1:18.]

- **Jesus' death released life on the earth.** *Christ Jesus, who has destroyed death and has brought life and immortality to light."* (2 Timothy 1:10)

Matthew 27:51–53 also describes the signs that happened when Jesus died, showing how this life could not be contained!

To do these things, Jesus had to be both true man and true God. First, he had to fulfill the law as a man in order to win us the righteousness gained by it (Galatians 4:4–5). He also had to be a man in order to suffer, die, and shed his blood. (Hebrews 9:22 says, "Without the shedding of blood there is no forgiveness.") Yet he had to also be God—Psalm 49:7 says that "no man can redeem the life of another." Only by dying as both man and God could he bring redemption to the world.

If there had been another way to bring redemption to the world, God would have found it. On the Mount of Olives before his death, Jesus cried out to God for another way, but there was none (Luke 22:42). In this day, it seems in vogue to believe there is more than one way to God—believing Jesus is the only way seems exclusive and narrow minded. Yet Jesus said he is the only way (John 14:6). And the cross was the only way for him. To believe anything else really is to belittle the price Jesus paid.

Justification

This section deals with how we become justified (declared righteous) and therefore saved. God has made it possible for us to be certain that salvation is ours and that we will be with him forever. Whether through Jesus' encounters with people such as the thief on the cross (Luke 23:40-43) or Paul's eloquent logic in Romans 4-10, God gives us total assurance we are saved the moment we turn to him in all honesty and ask to be part of his Kingdom.

First, as we saw above, this is only possible because of what Jesus went through on the cross. (This is called objective justification.) But we must personally receive it by faith (which is called subjective justification). It is of life-or-death importance that we know about this. Paul makes it very clear:

- **We have been saved by grace through faith.** *For it is by grace you have been saved, through faith—and this not from yourselves, it is the gift of God—not by works, so that no one can boast.* (Ephesians 2:8-9) [See also Romans 10:10 and John 3:16-18.]

First of all, this verse affirms that God's grace, in giving us what Jesus' death accomplished on the cross, is what saves us. But to receive it, we need faith. It says, however, that even having faith is not our own doing—the Holy Spirit supplies it (1 Corinthians 12:3,

Hebrews 12:2). Any work we do is simply not responsible for this—we can boast of nothing about ourselves that helps us be saved. Hence I call the cross the **great equalizer**—we are all in the same boat, falling dreadfully short of having earned God's favor ourselves, and we all come to salvation by sheer grace.

In understanding justification, it is important to understand faith. With faith, there is a "believing that" and "believing in." We believe *that* Jesus died for our sins, which is vital. But James 2:19 says "believing that" is not enough. We must also believe *in*. What we believe in is always God. This faith is heartfelt and personal (Romans 10:10). It is really a relationship with God—a relationship of trust. It is putting ourselves in his hands, all the while believing he will do what he promised.

> When we receive salvation, the Holy Spirit does something deep within.

When we receive salvation, the Holy Spirit does something deep within. The words of God's promises are brought to light in our minds, he creates faith in our hearts, and we turn from our old ways of life to something new: forgiveness, life, making Jesus our King. The word "repentance," so often found in verses about receiving salvation (Acts 2:38, etc.), connotes the turning of our minds from the old to the new. We are sorry for the old, and it may seem unbelievable that God would exchange that for something so good. This turning often seems like the bravest thing we have ever done. We are leaving behind the old and entering, by trust, into a new life, although we don't know exactly what that will be like. It's somewhat like running through a wall of fire without really knowing what is on the other side. But on the other side we will find we are now under the lordship of the best King imaginable, finding true life, true light, true freedom, and a God who loves us unceasingly. It may well be a hard life at times, but one that makes our old life seem shallow, lifeless, and without a cause.

III. OUR LIVES ON EARTH

God does not simply save us and leave us on earth just to bide our time until we go to heaven. Right here and right now he is active within us, changing us, and using us. We are set on an incredible adventure of walking with him.

Sanctification

I begin this section with a seeming contradiction to Ephesians 2:8–9 (quoted above) which tells us we have been saved by faith and not by works. James 2:24–26 says, "You see that a person is justified by what he does and not by faith alone. . . . Faith without deeds is dead." One of the things about faith is that it is living and will produce fruit (John 15:5). Someone once likened it to a golf swing: saving faith, lit within us by the Holy Spirit, is like the swing and hitting the ball is like the moment of salvation. Salvation is not because of what we do. Our deeds, which are the fruit of our faith and salvation, are like the follow-through to the swing. It would be as hard to stop the fruit as it is to hit a golf ball with no follow-through. The faith that brings us to salvation is the same faith which produces fruit. So James is looking at the complete swing to determine whether our faith is merely a mental assent that has no effect on our lives, or is alive, whereby we put ourselves into God's hands, leading us to fruitful places.

After our point of salvation, the Holy Spirit is at work in us to make us more like Jesus. He will give us an increasing distaste for sin (Romans 8:5), more freedom from what holds us back (2 Corinthians 3:17), a better character (Colossians 1:8), a stronger faith (2 Corinthians 1:21–22), a deeper knowing of God (Ephesians 1:17), more fruit of the Spirit (Galatians 5:22–23), and more effectiveness in what we do for God (1 Corinthians 12:4–6). This is the process of sanctification. Whereas justification was instantaneous and was a work of God, sanctification is lifelong and requires us and the Holy Spirit working together (Galatians 5:25).

CHAPTER 8

In chapter 3, I offered a detailed look at John 14, seeing how we partner together with God. There were also verses in that passage about obeying God. It makes you wonder: If God works in us through grace and by living within us (which is all his doing), how does our obedience fit into the picture? I have found that by not obeying what he wants us to do, we can shut off the flow of his work in us. There was a period of time when I knew God wanted me to do two things: I put them on my "to do" list, did everything but those two things, wrote another "to do" list, still did not do those two things, and on it went. Finally when I did those two things, it was as if the faucet of God had been turned on—I felt his flow again in many areas of my life. We can't expect God to flow through us if we keep turning off the faucet!

> Our walk with God is an adventure, and although the process of sanctification is painful at times, I have found it more freeing than burdensome.

Our walk with God is an adventure, and although the process of sanctification is painful at times, I have always found it more freeing than burdensome. I have also learned some things along the way that made the process easier. First, don't keep staring at yourself to see how your holiness is doing. Look to God (Hebrews 12:2). We become like the one we look at. Second, know the difference between condemnation and conviction. The enemy condemns us (Revelation 12:10), and his purpose is to draw us away from God. Conviction is different—when the Holy Spirit convicts us of sin, the result will be to empower us and draw us close to God. Isaiah 6:1–8 is a beautiful example of how this works: Isaiah was convicted but ended up wanting to be sent by the Lord. Third, if you want grace and forgiveness in your own life (which you do!), give grace and forgiveness to others (Luke 6:36–38). There are, of course, many more things to say about furthering the process of sanctification. Paul always ends his letters with such advice, and the entire

Bible was written to move us forward in the process of knowing, being like, and becoming closer to God.

Carrying Our Crosses

When Christians talk about the cross, they may be talking about one of two things: the cross that Jesus died upon to take away our sins or the cross that we are to carry in our lives (Luke 9:23), referring to the sacrifices we make for him. We must not confuse the two by thinking that the cross we willingly carry for his sake (which is indeed precious to him) will earn our salvation or anyone else's. Only what happened on his cross can do that.

In Luke 9:23 Jesus said that a believer "must take up his cross daily." Right after these words, it is interesting to see how many verses there are about how he was headed toward his own cross (Luke 9:31, 44, 51, 62). It is also interesting how the disciples (like us!) were so slow to get the message of carrying their crosses. Within these very same verses they argued about who was the greatest (Luke 9:46), tried to stop others from doing God's work because they were not disciples (Luke 9:49–50), and even asked Jesus if they should call down fire from heaven on a village that did not welcome them (Luke 9:53–56). Eventually they got it. In fact tradition has it that all but one died martyrs' deaths because of their dedication to Jesus:

- † James: beheaded by Herod in Jerusalem.
- † James the Less: crucified in Egypt or thrown from a pinnacle.
- † Andrew: crucified on St. Andrew's cross.
- † Jude: martyred in Persia.
- † Philip: martyred in Phrygia.
- † Nathaniel: flayed to death.
- † Matthew: martyred in Ethiopia.

- † Thomas: shot by arrows while at prayer.
- † Simon the Zealot: crucified.
- † Simon Peter: crucified upside down in Rome.
- † John: banished to Patmos, recalled, and died a natural death.

Like the firemen who died on 9/11, they did not want to die—they simply wanted to help those in trouble and laid down their lives because of their love for people and dedication to their calls. Once we determine that our lives are his, then we will have come far in slaying our inner resistance toward serving him, loving others, and going where he tells us to go.

The Church

The church (Greek: *ekklesia*, meaning "called out ones") refers to all who have received his gift of salvation—all Christians. Jesus also refers to the church as his body:

- **We are one body.** *In Christ we who are many form one body, and each member belongs to all the others.* (Romans 12:5)

The Church, then, is comprised of believers found in every local church and every denomination. Jesus prayed for the unity of all believers in John 17:20–23. I don't know that this necessitates the disbanding of denominations, but it certainly is talking about a love for all believers that we need to have within our hearts. Maybe we can even think of the different denominations as analogous to the different branches of the armed services, each having their areas of specialization—in a time of war, everyone appreciates the role of every branch and feels a camaraderie with one another, knowing they all have the same cause and the same commander in chief.

- **It is important to meet together.** *Let us not give up meeting together.* (Hebrews 10:25)

Although we initially come to the Lord as individuals, there is something important about meeting together in groups. Jesus promised that his presence would be manifested in a special way when we do (Matthew 18:20). Also, as we come together it is as if we are building something out of living stones, each having a special place. We are holy priests within it (1 Peter 2:5). Scripture says there is a strength when we join together (Matthew 18:19, Deuteronomy 32:30) and the gates of hell—which hold the world in captivity—won't prevail when we storm them as a body (Matthew 16:18).

Granted, it is not always easy rubbing shoulders with those odd people in Christ's body. In solitude we can fool ourselves into thinking our sanctification is well under way, but in reality it needs to be tested among other people. Jesus came up with the perfect place for us to be vigorously tested: the church! Here sanctification is tested by how well we express love and unity (Colossians 3:12–14). Here iron can sharpen iron as we all grow together (Proverbs 27:17). There are incredible blessings in being with our family in God; there is nothing like the support and friendship we can find there if we press through our difficulties and differences.

IV. OUR LIVES IN HEAVEN

While some wish the Bible described heaven in even more detail, it says enough that we know heaven is a place of extreme wonder. For me, it is enough to know that that's where God will be (2 Corinthians 5:8). But Jesus also describes it as paradise (Luke 23:43). Psalm 16:11 (KJV) says that in God's presence is fullness of joy. Revelation goes into some vivid and unusual descriptions of what it looks like. One of the most unforgettable:

- **No more tears.** *Now the dwelling of God is with men, and he will live with them. They will be his people, and God himself will be with them and be their God. He will wipe every tear from their eyes. There will be no more death or mourning or crying or pain, for the old order of things has passed away.* (Revelation 21:3–4)

No wonder Revelation 14:13 says, "Blessed are the dead who die in the Lord from now on."

> They will be his people and God himself will be with them and be their God.

Some wonder, what happens the moment we die? From the story Jesus told about the rich man and Lazarus (Luke 16:19–31), it seems we are active and recognize others. Luke 23:43 says we will experience heaven immediately: "Today you will be with me in paradise." And he said of Abraham, Isaac, and Jacob, their God is "not the God of the dead, but of the living," indicating they are living right now in heaven.

Jesus' Resurrection and Ours

In dazzling reality, the resurrection of Jesus (1 Corinthians 15:3–6) revealed what his death on the cross had accomplished. His atonement was accepted as the sacrifice for our sins (Romans 4:25). He demonstrated the victory of life now reigning over death (1 Corinthians 15:54). He was enthroned over all, above every title that could be given (Ephesians 1:19–23).

The resurrection was also a declaration that, since he lives, we, too, shall live.

- **We shall live.** *Jesus said to her, "I am the resurrection and the life. He who believes in me shall live, even though he*

dies; and whoever lives and believes in me will never die."
(John 11:25–26) [See also John 14:19.]

There will come a time when those who are in heaven and those who are on earth will experience something equally as dazzling. On the last day (John 6:39)—the day when Jesus returns—the atoms which were once part of our bodies will be summoned to make a transformation into new bodies for us. In our flesh we will see God (Job 19:25–27). But this will not be ordinary flesh and bones:

> "I am the resurrection and the life."

- **Our resurrected bodies will be glorified.** *The body that is sown is perishable, it is raised imperishable; . . . it is sown a natural body, it is raised a spiritual body.* (1 Corinthians 15:42b,44) [See all of 1 Corinthians 15:35–58, Philippians 3:21, and 1 John 3:2.]

We will have bodies like Jesus' body, which defied the laws of nature (John 20:19) and never will know decay (Psalm 16:10). A new order will come into being (Revelation 21:1–5)—a new heaven and earth will be known. And, beginning with the wedding feast between us and the Lamb, that is where we will live, always with him.

Jesus' Second Coming and the End Times

Jesus will come back to earth a second time.

- **Jesus will come again.** *This same Jesus . . . will come back in the same way you have seen him go into heaven.* (Acts 1:11) [See also Revelation 1:7, Matthew 25:31.]

We don't know when this will happen (Matthew 24:36), although there will be signs the time is near and it will be a time of great tribulation (See all of Matthew 24). Peter felt it was near (1 Peter 4:7) and it is now even closer for us than it was for him.

There are two other events Christians sometimes talk about when discussing the end times. One is what is called the *Rapture*, when those on earth will be taken up to be with Jesus at the time when the dead are resurrected (1 Thessalonians 4:17). The second is what is called the *Millennium*, a thousand-year reign with Jesus on earth as described in Revelation 20:1–6. There are differences of opinion as to the timing of these things. Premillennialists believe the Second Coming is before the Millennium, postmillennialists say it is after. Amillennialists say the Millennium is a prophetic description of the age between the first and Second Comings of Jesus. Then there are pre-tribulationists who say the Rapture happens before the Tribulation and post-tribulationists who say it happens after. What is truly important, however, is to be looking to the Lord and doing all he told us to do before he comes.

Final Judgment

On the last day, when Jesus returns, he will judge all who are living and all who have died.

- **Jesus will judge all.** *For we must all appear before the judgment seat of Christ, . . .* (2 Corinthians 5:10) [See also Acts 17:31.]

Although the works of all will be judged, some found to be like gold and others like straw (1 Corinthians 3:12–15), it is clear that what counts for our salvation is our faith in Jesus.

- **We are saved by believing in Jesus.** *For God so loved the world that he gave his one and only Son, that whoever believes in him shall not perish but have eternal life. . . . Whoever believes in the Son has eternal life, but whoever rejects the Son will not see life."* (John 3:16, 36)

Hell is not a popular subject these days, but Jesus warned about it often. It would be to our detriment and the detriment of others to ignore it. Some wonder how a loving God could send people to hell. Others try to scare people into heaven by frightening them about hell, turning the Good News into scary news. However, the fact of man heading toward hell is not news at all; it has been happening all along by our own doing. The verses in John 3 quoted above show how God's love prompted him to do something about it. There was only one way out of it for us, and God gave everything he had that we may have that way out. That is amazing news.

Embracing Mystery

Some people seem to want to explain everything in the Bible and have every question answered. The truth is that the Bible leaves many things unexplained. You only need to look at how much it leaves unsaid about heaven to see this. Sometimes the best (and most honest) thing to do is just to embrace its mystery and know that one day God will show us more when we are with him in heaven.

> Sometimes the best thing to do is just to embrace its mystery.

One area of mystery is when verses seem to contradict each other. Sometimes there is a gold mine of understanding to be had when you dig into the seeming contradiction. Other times it remains a mystery. For instance, there are some verses that say those who are saved were predestined to be saved (such as Ephesians 1:5), yet other verses that say God desires all to be saved (such as 1 Timothy 2:4). Both are true. To me, predestination is somewhat like trying to understand how time travel might work—I simply don't know. I'm sure in heaven we will see how God knew all along who would come to him, and we will give him full credit for choosing us and predestining us to be there. Yet it is certainly true that God desires all to be saved—that is God's heart which is reiterated throughout Scripture, and we can tell that to an individual who may be thinking, "Jesus may have died for a lot of people, but he would never die for me." Yes, he did die for you, and he wants you in his Kingdom. He really does want to gather us all up under his wings.

V. THE WORD OF GOD

The Bible acknowledges that we can know some things about God through nature (Romans 1:20)—things that should cause us to seek after God (Acts 17:27). But much that is to be known about God he has chosen to reveal only through his Word (1 Corinthians 2:9–13).

His Word shows us what is truly on his heart. It shows us the way to salvation; it thoroughly equips us (2 Timothy 3:15–17). The Word is powerful. It produces faith (Romans 10:17). It is endued with the ability to accomplish that for which it was written:

- **The Word will not return empty.** *My word that goes out from my mouth: It will not return to me empty, but will accomplish what I desire and achieve the purpose for which I sent it."* (Isaiah 55:11)

> His promises are as powerful today as when he first spoke them.

In other words, the Word has the very power of God still ringing in it from when he originally spoke it or had it written (Hebrews 4:12). We live in a temporal world, whereas the things of God are eternal. When we speak, our words go out and disappear. When God speaks, his words do not fade away but remain forever. So his promises are as powerful today as when he first spoke them.

Note: The eternal aspect of God shows up in his Word in fascinating ways. I already mentioned how prophetic Scriptures often bounced between the three mountain peaks of foreseeing the days soon to come and Jesus' first and second comings. Also, from God's perspective of being outside of time, we often see his words and actions not only reflecting past events, but reflecting future events. For example, when Jesus died on the cross, the resurrection power released coincided with an earthquake and people being raised from the dead: a "foreshock" of the resurrection power that was to raise Jesus from the dead two days later (Matthew 27:51-53). This timeless point of view can also be seen in the "bookends" surrounding various accounts in Scripture. For example, the entire Bible itself begins with a description of the Garden of Eden (with a river, trees, and God's presence) and then ends in Revelation 22 with a very similar description of heaven. In the Garden, we see man hiding from God; in Revelation 22, after the redemptive story throughout all the Bible's pages, we now see Jesus' bride crying out, "Come!" Also interesting is how this description of heaven is so similar to the flow of the Spirit described in Ezekiel 47; it foreshadows Jesus' ministry (and ours) as the Kingdom of heaven touches the earth—his will being done on earth as it is in heaven—the future being experienced in the "now."

How the Word Was Written

Scripture states that the Bible is the word of God, yet man had a role in writing it:

- **The Bible is the Word of God.** *When you received the word of God, which you heard from us, you accepted it not as the word of men, but as it actually is, the word of God, which is at work in you who believe.* (1 Thessalonians 2:13)

- **It was written by people as they were moved by the Holy Spirit.** *For prophecy never had its origin in the will of man, but men spoke from God as they were carried along by the Holy Spirit.* (2 Peter 1:21)

Second Timothy 3:16 says that "all Scripture is God-breathed." In other words, God breathed his direction upon the writers, yet their styles, backgrounds, and experiences still came through in the writing as they participated in this remarkable partnership with God. Clearly it pleased him to have the styles and personalities of the diverse authors flavor each individual work. Hence we believe the Scriptures to be diverse in authorship, style, and form, yet unified by being God's word, written just as he wanted it to be written.

The Integrity of the Word

- **The Word is truth.** *Your word is truth.* (John 17:17)

The way most of the church expresses its belief in the Bible's integrity is by stating it is "inerrant in its original manuscripts." It is said in this way to deal with the many small variations in the copies of the text we now have. (We don't have the originals.) Acknowledging how those variations are small and produce no differences in what we believe, I would even go beyond the usual concept of the Bible's integrity and express how the Word is precious to God and how he has been hovering over it all these years to bring it to us in purity. He also hovered over the acceptance of the books into the Canon (those that are accepted as being part of the Bible), made official in the fourth century (although most of the books were thought of as Scripture years before that). Regarding the Canon, Hebrews 1:1–2 shows us that the revelation spoken to us by God's Son is the ultimate in what we believe about God; hence the church holds to a belief that the Canon is complete.

Baptism and Communion

The Word can be read, spoken, or heard, all with its innate power intact. The Word can also be expressed in action. Two such actions instituted by Jesus are baptism and Communion.

The action of baptism is beautiful. The descent into water is analogous to being buried with Jesus, and rising up out of it to being resurrected with him (Romans 6:4). We realize how our sins have been washed away (Ephesians 5:26) as we make an entrance into a new life. This Word-in-action is deeply personal and powerful.

This also applies to the action of Communion. It is telling us that Jesus' body, broken on the cross for the sins of the world, was broken for me—given to me up close and personal. So it is with the blood of the New Covenant—it was poured out and is a covenant also with me (Luke 22:19-20).

Communion, as personal as it is, also has a community aspect—we are embracing him, but as part of one another (1 Corinthians 11:17-34). The same thing is true of baptism. We are becoming part of, and becoming embraced by, the church—Christians everywhere share in our blessing.

At some point in the history of the church, people came to discuss the words about the body and blood (as it pertains to the bread and cup) in Communion (the "Real Presence"). Some thought of it as a molecular change (which is not in the spirit of John 6:63), some described it in Aristotelian terms, some said it was purely symbolic, some left it a mystery. We do know that Jesus promised to be with us: always and as we gather together (Matthew 28:20, 18:20). Regardless of how we view the bread and cup, therefore, we can savor his being with us as we commune with him.

Likewise there has been a debate over how and when to administer baptism, particularly whether or not to baptize infants. Some say individuals have to be old enough to know what they are doing. Others say that even the littlest of children should come to Jesus, citing that entire households believed and were baptized (Acts 16:33). Early church history has references supporting both points of view (not that it is authoritative, just interesting). I know and respect vibrant Christians on both sides of this issue.

CHAPTER 8

Law and Grace

Second Timothy 2:15 (NKJV) speaks of "rightly dividing the word of truth." Often Scripture has several things to say on a given subject, and it is up to us to bring in the appropriate one. To decide, we must have the heart of God on the matter.

Martin Luther applied this verse to divide the Scriptures that speak of the law from those that speak of grace. Both law and grace are good, but we need an understanding of what they do and how to use them. The law is basically "you should" and "you should not" statements. It can also carry the consequences of disobeying it. The law can curb society (1 Timothy 1:9), act as our guide (Psalm 119:9–10), or act as a mirror, telling us how desperately we need Jesus (Romans 3:20). Grace is basically what God does on our behalf. It may be getting the good things we do not deserve or not getting the bad things we do deserve (mercy). What Jesus has done for us is the ultimate in grace and mercy.

The law can be used as a knife (Hebrews 4:12) to cut away the thoughts and attitudes of our heart that are opposed to what God says is good. This can be lifesaving in the right hands (like those of a surgeon), but in the wrong hands (like those of a criminal) the very same knife can condemn, remove hope, or wreak destruction.

In Galatians 3 Paul says that there are limitations on what the law can do. It cannot earn us salvation or God's acceptance. Nor does it have the power to fulfill what it demands. Only grace can do these things. Therefore we can't try to use the law for what only grace can do.

> **In Galatians 3 Paul says that there are limitations on what the law can do.**

Both law and grace are needed. Without the law we could slip into the false idea that God could not possibly punish sin or merely winks at moral failure (unsanctified mercy). Also, without the law people may not know their need for God: "Why should I receive grace or mercy if everything's going well in my life?"

Without grace (or the Holy Spirit) we can try to motivate out of fear or guilt. Without grace we can end up in legalism, where we either fool ourselves into believing we have earned God's favor through fulfilling the law, or we are in despair because we keep trying to gain acceptance through what we do and keep failing. Without grace we will lack the power that people need to be saved, know the acceptance of God, or be freed from sin.

Therefore we need both law and grace. When teaching, know what to use when. Know the power of each, and use them accordingly and with skill. Most importantly, seek God to know his heart. We need the heart of a good shepherd, desiring to restore and not merely shove people away out of an intolerance for imperfection. Basically we need to pray, asking God to show us the situation our people are in and what truth will best set them on the course toward life.

THEOLOGY FOR LIFE ISSUES

There are theological discussions which are not often covered in systematic theology textbooks that people really need to understand in order to handle issues that come up in their lives. Without such discussions, we leave people on their own to come up with ideas that are sometimes mistaken or incomplete.

A Theology of Troubles

Sometimes when people find themselves beset by troubles, they either give up or think God is mad at them. God must have felt it was important to have a good "theology of troubles," since perhaps the first book penned was the book of Job, which deals with this head on.

CHAPTER 8

It is important to realize that often we do not know why troubles have come. In the book of Job, the readers know what was going on behind the scenes in heaven, but throughout the book Job never knew! Sometimes we must simply embrace the mystery of it. Giving pat answers to those in trouble is often less than helpful.

Job's counselors told Job he must have done something wrong or that God was displeased with him (Job 4:7, 8:4, 11:5). Although we sometimes end up in trouble by our own doing, this is not always the case (especially when we are sick or have endured tragedy) and was certainly not the case here. Scripture records God's harsh words for Job's counselors (Job 42:7). God's words to Job were that his ways are often simply too much for us to comprehend (Job 42:3) and call for trust without always having understanding.

David's psalms are classics in heart attitudes when troubles beset us. In the first two verses of Psalm 3 (NJKV), David describes how his enemies rose up against him and how so many said, "There is no help for him in God." Then his eyes went to the Lord and the rest of the Psalm is a proclamation of praise and faith in how much help there really is in God. The change within the Psalm is so dramatic that many liberal scholars think two people wrote it. They are right: David before his eyes were on the Lord and David after his eyes were on the Lord! Sometimes we must enter into the "sacrifice of praise" and praise him even when circumstances are telling us not to.

People's "theologies of troubles" can fall into one of two ditches: They can think God's people will never have any troubles, or they can think that once they do have them, there is no help for them in God. Both Psalm 34:19 and John 16:33 come against these ideas head-on. Both verses testify that the righteous may indeed have troubles in this world, but there *is* help in God. We have someone on our side: God our Deliverer, who has overcome the world. Look to him. God is for us! And he is mighty to help and to save.

A Theology of Healing

Closely tied to a "theology of troubles" is a theology of healing. Again we have the two ditches of thinking that God's people will never succumb to sickness (if they do everything right) or thinking that God will rarely do anything supernatural to heal us. The latter is often thinly disguised by people who pray, "If it be thy will, heal this person." In reality, they have no faith that God's will is to answer such a prayer. We need to read Scripture to see what God's will, in general, for healing is! Looking at the ministry of Jesus, we know God loves to heal—both out of compassion and to demonstrate that his Kingdom has come—although we may not always know the when or the how.

Isaiah 53:5 (and Matthew 8:17) speaks of healing in the atonement. While it is good to explore the depths of what this means, it was not intended to give us a theology of healing that is so rigid as to exclude healing from the unsaved or cause the sick who are saved to doubt their faith or salvation. Scripture does neither of these things. Following the example of Jesus, God often uses us to heal unbelievers—something that contributed to the explosive growth of the early church. Rather than our adopting a rules-based approach to when God should and should not heal, God, who is wonderfully creative and caring, wants to partner with us in bringing healing—which can come at any time to anyone, that they may know his goodness.

So where do we turn for a theology of healing? Turning to the ministry of Jesus, where healing was a commonplace occurrence, we find an excellent fit for healing in the theology of the Kingdom of God. With the exception of the work of theologians like George Eldon Ladd, it is surprising how underutilized the Kingdom of God has been in forming a theology. Jesus spoke of it often—in the Gospels it is mentioned over one hundred times.

Previously I mentioned how the kingdom of the enemy is characterized by deceit, darkness, disease, bondage, and death, but the

Kingdom of God is characterized by truth, light, health, freedom, and life. Often the kingdoms clashed, with the Kingdom of God obliterating the kingdom of darkness, and the sick, oppressed, and deceived remarkably set free. The Kingdom was proclaimed in what Jesus said; it was demonstrated in the works he did. The coming of the Kingdom, in all its beauty and freedom, was often manifested in tangible ways, and healing was one of those ways. It displayed the heart of the King.

Note: I am using physical healing as an example here. However, I could just as well use another category of healing, such as the healing of emotions and past hurts, healing of relationships, or healing of something that affects a person's relationship with God. Social maladies like abuse, neglect, and drug dependence are at epidemic proportions today and there is an overwhelming need for healing of all kinds. George Koch, in his upcoming book on healing prayer, points out that those who have been sinned against (in contrast with those sinning) are often neglected, but Jesus desires to bring healing to them (Luke 4:18–19). George writes, "Sin is not victimless, but the church in large measure has been devoted to the redemption of sinners and often oblivious to the victims of sin. The Gospel is also for the victims of sin, and it promises redemption and healing for them." His book is devoted to ways to bring them that healing.

One question we might ask is this: is the Kingdom now or not yet? Verses such as Matthew 8:11 talk of the Kingdom as coming on the last day (when it will come in its fullness); others such as Luke 10:9 talk of it as happening now. Therefore both are true; the Kingdom is both now and not yet. It is as if the Kingdom of the future is constantly breaking forth into the "now"— heaven is touching earth. We don't know where the Kingdom is going to burst out next, but it is its nature to do so. When Jesus was on earth, he was the point man of a

> We don't know where the Kingdom is going to burst out next, but it is its nature to do so.

heavenly invasion: his Kingdom was breaking in. Now we are its point men and women. He has called *us* to ask the Kingdom to come.

With healing, therefore, we pray with utter confidence, "Your Kingdom come." (Matthew 6:10). (In the Greek this is in the imperative: "Kingdom, come!") Jesus is giving us the authority and mandate to do this. And when we ask his presence and Kingdom to come, we follow God's cue in however healing, freedom, and life burst forth. It's up to him exactly what will happen, but what he does is often better than what we can think or imagine. Is faith needed? Yes. But he often gives us what we need when we need it—sometimes the very moment we pray for the sick, he speaks to us what he is about to do, an intense faith wells in our hearts, and we see healing come.

This, then, gives us a theology of healing. It does not set in concrete exactly what God is going to do in every circumstance (that is up to him), but it does give us a confidence that he loves to heal and loves to demonstrate that the Kingdom has come. We don't know where the Kingdom is going to burst out next, but Jesus taught us to expectantly speak for it to do so. Like Jesus, who only did what he saw the Father doing (John 5:19), we also partner with God as we experience his presence and see his works unfold. And we find that he loves to use us to bring his Kingdom and healing to those who need it.

(For more on this subject, see my first book: *The Presence, Power and Heart of God—Partnering in His Ministry*.)

OTHER MAJORS OF THE FAITH

When I took systematic theology I found it odd—and somewhat frustrating—that although it did cover our lives on earth with regard to sanctification, it did not talk about our being used here on earth for God's work. This is especially bizarre since so much of the New Testament shows Jesus doing his work and teaching others to do the same. If God devoted so much attention to this, then so should we. We should equip our people to be equippers and doers. Whatever we learn as pastors and leaders, we should turn around and give it to others so they, too, can do and lead.

Our Call to the Ministry of Jesus

I touched upon our call to the ministry of Jesus in the previous section. Recall how first Jesus, and now we, are called to be precipitators of the Kingdom of God. Also recall chapter 3 where we looked at John 14 describing how we partner with God—there we saw how we also partner with him in his works. In all of these places, our ministering with Jesus can range from the everyday to the supernatural, from serving to prophesying, from hospitality to healing. God wants to do it all and wants us to partner with him in doing it. Now we turn to the book of Acts which describes how our ministry is empowered by the Holy Spirit.

In the opening verses of Acts, Luke writes, "In my former book [the Gospel of Luke], Theophilus, I wrote about all that Jesus *began* [emphasis mine] to do and teach until the day he was taken up to heaven." (Acts 1:1–2) Using the word "began" implies that Luke's second book described what Jesus *continued* to do. But after he rose to heaven, what he continued to do was through his empowered disciples, which includes you and me.

Before he ascended, however, Jesus told his disciples to wait for the coming of the Holy Spirit:

> *Do not leave Jerusalem, but wait for the gift my Father promised, which you have heard me speak about. For John baptized with water, but in a few days you will be baptized with the Holy Spirit.* (Acts 1:4–5)

This would empower them to be his witnesses (Acts 1:8)—and the entire book of Acts describes the ministry that empowered disciples can do. It was just like the ministry that Jesus did.

Descriptions of the Spirit first coming on people—which Jesus calls a baptism with the Holy Spirit—are depicted in Acts 2:1–41, 10:44–48 and 19:1–6. Theologically it is difficult for some to connect these verses to our lives because, for the people in Acts, it was the initial outpouring of the Spirit, whereas, for us, the Holy Spirit has been active a long time in our salvation and sanctification (although maybe not as it is described in the aforementioned verses). However, we don't have to deny that the Spirit has been with us already to desire more. He wants us to desire more! (See Hebrews 11:6, 1 Corinthians 14:1, Psalm 42:1) If you have not experienced anything like the baptisms of the Holy Spirit in the book of Acts, ask for it. How certainly will he give the Holy Spirit to those who ask (Luke 11:13)!

So what is it like when the Holy Spirit comes in this way? It is common to experience his gifts (Acts 19:6), his fruit, such as a profound sense of peace or joy (Galatians 5:22–23), and his presence (Acts 4:31). We are often launched into a deepened pursuit of God, a love for worship (Ephesians 5:18–19), and longing for true holiness (Galatians 5:16), finding ourselves captivated by him and more disinterested in the lures of the world. We are launched into a closeness with him (John 14:16), a love for his works and ways (Acts 1:8), an impartation of his character, and a joyful willingness to embrace the type of brokenness where God chooses to dwell (Isaiah 57:15, Luke 4:1). Above all, he becomes our best friend. We enter the joy of knowing him, realizing how close he is, listening to his voice, learning as he illuminates the Word, and hearing him tell us what he is doing in our lives and in the world around us (John 16:13). And this

> **This closeness—this partnering with him— is how God brings us into a life of Spirit-led ministry.**

closeness—this partnering with him—is how God brings us into a life of Spirit-led ministry.

Let me say a few things about hearing from God. The Bible, of course, is the main means of hearing from God. It is his clear and undisputed voice and our sole source of doctrine. However, we often need specific direction for specific situations, especially when we want to "do what we see the Father doing" (John 5:19) in ministry settings. The Word was not written with the intent of listing step-by-step instructions for every circumstance we might ever encounter. (That's probably not even possible and, if it were, in the natural realm we often don't know what all the circumstances are.) The Bible does give us general instructions, but it also portrays God as one who will speak to us about specific details in our lives and show us the way. Looking at his relationship with Moses and David, for example, we can see that he loves his people close to him, praying, asking, talking, and listening to his voice. He wants us to draw close. Scripture contains over twenty-one hundred verses showing God speaking to people in various ways. As in any relationship, communication is important. Can you imagine a relationship without it, or one in which one partner did all the talking and the other only listened? God both speaks and listens, and he often wants to speak to us or to strengthen, encourage, or comfort others through us (1 Corinthians 14:3). He told us twice to earnestly desire to prophesy (1 Corinthians 14:1,39), in which we both hear from him and speak what he says to others.

We, in partnership with God, will minister like Jesus to a hurting world, no matter if we are doing the mundane or miraculous, the small or the big. As we go out into the world, we will bring his presence, see his power, and have his heart beating in ours. There is nothing quite like ministering with God, and to do so is the call and privilege of us all (1 Peter 2:9).

Our Call to Love and Worship

In Matthew 22:36–40 Jesus summarized the law this way: "'Love the Lord your God with all your heart and with all your soul and with all your mind.'" and "'Love your neighbor as yourself.' All the Law and the Prophets hang on these two commands." By "Law and Prophets" he was referring to the Old Testament—these two commands encapsulate what the Old Testament is about.

In chapter 2 we looked at the major themes of the Old Testament. One theme was "Knowing God," which we found to include an intimate, personal, loving relationship with him. In his first command, Jesus reiterates this by a call to love God with all that is within us. Another theme was "Living as God's People" and this, Jesus often said, is fulfilled by loving others. That is what he is saying in his second command. (In John 5:39 he also affirms the third theme, "The Promised Messiah," when he speaks of Old Testament Scripture as testifying about himself.)

One way to live out our love for God is through worship. It is not as though God is vain and needs to be told how good he is. Rather, worship is stepping into the reality of how good he is—the reality where all creation sings of his wonder and excellence. Although music is but one way we can express our worship, musical worship is a remarkable gift and can carry a heavenly anointing in which God inhabits our praises (Psalm 22:3, NKJV).

> **Worship is stepping into the reality of how good God is . . . where all creation sings of his wonder and excellence.**

The dimensions of musical worship can be seen in some of the words used to describe it. In the space of several verses in Psalm 33, it is interesting how many Hebrew words denoting worship are used:

CHAPTER 8

Sing joyfully [**ranah**: shout for joy] *to the* LORD *you righteous; it is fitting for the upright to praise* [**hallel**: demonstrative praise—often boastful, noisy or clamorously foolish] *him. Praise* [**yadah**: praise with outstretched arms] *the* LORD *with the harp; make music* [**zamar**: make music in praise to God] *to him on the ten-stringed lyre. Sing* [**shyr**: sing, like a strolling minstrel] *to him a new song; play* [**nagan**: play, strike strings] *skillfully, and shout* [**teruw**: shout or blast a shofar] *for joy."*
(Psalm 33:1–3)

The New Testament, which extends our concepts of closeness to God, often depicts worship using the Greek word *proskuneo*, which connotes prostrating ourselves, adoring on one's knees, or turning toward to kiss.

The loving of God—Jesus' first command—then spills into Jesus' second command: to love our neighbors. This involves those closest to us: our spouses, children, and parents, and extends to those even in the uttermost parts of the earth. The ways we can do this are countless. The full creativity of God is at our disposal to show such love. God's love knew no bounds—it prompted him to give his very life (1 John 4:7–12)—so how certainly will he be with us as we show his love for the world.

It is fitting, having seen how Jesus summarized the Old Testament in two commands, to end our summary of theology. While not as brief as Jesus' statements, it is much more brief than most systematic theologies which cover more subjects and each one in vastly more detail.

Now we will use everything we have covered in the first eight chapters and see how to research and teach the amazing Word of God.

Thinking More About It

Ω Clearly, not all topics mentioned in Scripture can be covered in a systematic theology book. If you wanted to develop an understanding of a topic (take, for example, a Scriptural view of angels), how would you go about doing that?

Ω Remember that your theology is drawn from the Word, which must be your foundation. Lean on it versus your own understanding of it.

Ω Look up some of the Scripture references I gave in this chapter. Be a "Berean" and make sure what I was saying is in agreement with those supporting verses. Also write down other supporting verses as you come across them so you have references ready should you ever teach on any of these subjects.

CHAPTER NINE

How to Research the Word

While the next chapter addresses how to teach the Word, this chapter will discuss how to research the Word as if we were preparing to teach on one particular text.

On the next page, you will see a list of twelve steps that are useful for doing a study on a specific text. For a given verse, you will find that some of these steps may not yield a lot, while other steps may lead to gold mines. Since it is not always obvious which will yield the most fruit, it is best to go through them all. In this chapter I will expand on each step and also give an example which illustrates how that step can add to your teaching.

PREPARATION

Before you do any of this, of course, you need to find the text you wish to teach on. Maybe it is one the Lord has highlighted as you were reading it. Perhaps you are working your way through a book of the Bible, and it's your turn to teach on the next verses. Or maybe there is a subject you are interested in, and you have found a verse which speaks into it.

Before you dig into the verse, pray that the Lord would reveal and highlight what he wants to say to you through it, so that as you go through the steps, you would develop a teaching containing both the truth and heart of God that will impact the hearts of your listeners. Partner with him in it.

Steps for Textual Bible Studies

As you read over your verse, pray that God would reveal and highlight what he wants to tell you.

I. Setting—What is the setting of the text? What is the relationship of this text to the themes and setting of the book?

II. Feeling—Put yourself in the shoes of the people in the passage or of the original hearers. How do you feel?

III. Text—Look at several translations. Look at individual words. Look up key words in a lexicon (such as *Vine*).

IV. Immediate Context—Are there any connections with the texts immediately before and after your text?

V. Issues—List the spiritual truths you come across.

VI. Central Thought—What is the central thought of the text? What is the author's passion for writing the text? What is the central thought God wants to convey to your hearers?

VII. Related Texts—Find related texts and see how they shed light on your text.

VIII. Illustrations—What modern day experience illustrates this thought? Do any other Scripture passages or other quotes illustrate this thought?

IX. Application—What difference does (or should) this truth make in your life? What should we ask God to do in our lives in light of what we've discovered?

X. Commentaries—You may wish to check out commentaries, sermons, etc., to see what God has spoken to other people regarding this text.

XI. Organize—Trim your thoughts to what will impact your listeners the most. Keep your central thought central.

XII. Pray—God, what do you want to say to the people?

I. SETTING

Know who is speaking and who the listeners were. Know when and where the event takes place and why the words are being said, perhaps looking into what problems were present.

It can also be valuable to know the general setting of the book and the themes that run through it. That often sheds light on what the text is saying and why it is being said. In chapters 4 and 5, I gave a very brief summary of the settings for each book of the Bible. To get more information, many study Bibles give an interesting introduction at the beginning of each book. There are also a number of Old and New Testament surveys that do this in more detail.

In chapters 2 and 3, I talked about some of the themes that run through the entire Old and New Testaments. This is also helpful in showing how the text fits into the bigger picture. Sometimes, if there is a connection in your text with these settings or themes, it is a good opportunity to teach about them. This often inspires more interest to explore the Word.

Example: Report of the Ten Spies

All the people we saw there are of great size. . . . We seemed like grasshoppers in our own eyes, and we looked the same to them. (Numbers 13:32b–33)

This was a report from ten of the twelve spies sent to survey the land God had instructed his people to occupy. After hearing this, the people reacted in fear. These verses have a very important connection to the setting of the book. In Numbers, Moses was leading the people to the Promised Land. Then, because of their unbelief, they were left to wander in the wilderness for forty years. This passage is the turning point in that journey, showing how that unbelief started and manifested itself. They should have been looking at their circumstances through God's eyes, not their own. As God pointed out in

Numbers 14, all the miracles he did should have changed the way they saw things. So it is with us—God will give us "eyes of faith" if we ask. Without them we, too, will be blind to his awesome works and may end up walking in circles for a long, long time.

II. FEELING

It is always a good idea to put yourself in the shoes of the original hearers, the speaker, or even God himself to see how the incident being described impacts you. As I discussed in chapter 2, a passage is often written to impact our hearts, and we need to feel the ways it does this in order to convey its impact to those we teach.

Example: Taking up Our Crosses

> *Then Jesus said to his disciples, "If anyone would come after me, he must deny himself and take up his cross and follow me."* (Matthew 16:24)

Realize that Jesus said this *before* he was crucified upon the cross. So the original hearers received this differently than we often do, since we immediately think of the cross as a symbol of the Christian faith. To them all they knew about the cross was that it was an instrument of death. It would be like Jesus telling us that we must carry our own guillotine—quite a shock to the original hearers. This was a radical thing Jesus said—you can feel Jesus' passion as he tries to free us from the things that hold us back. In other words, we must decide now that we are giving our lives to his cause—this guillotine blade could come slamming down upon our comforts, our business-as-usual lifestyle, or even our lives at any time as we pursue our love for others and for God. So be free of the hold of these things *now*.

III. TEXT

Now we look at the text itself. First, look at it in several English translations. Some translations are very literal. The *King James Version* (KJV) keeps closest to the Greek or Hebrew text's word order. This gives it a poetic feel, although sometimes makes it hard to read. The *New King James Version* (NKJV) is like the *King James Version* but replaces some of the older English words (such as *thee* and *thou*) with the modern English counterparts. The *New International Version* (NIV) was created by a team of some of the best evangelical scholars across the world and ended up with a very accurate yet readable version of the Bible. There are many other excellent literal translations as well, such as the *New American Standard Bible* (NASB). There are also paraphrased translations, such as the *New Living Translation* or *The Message*. These take an entire sentence in the Greek or Hebrew and try to express its meaning with a very readable English sentence, although not necessarily matching word for word. I often find those interesting just to sit down and read. They sometimes bring out a meaning that the Greek is trying to convey that is a little less obvious in the other translations. While I would not lean on a paraphrase alone for a teaching, I often find it an interesting supplement and may quote it if it is particularly striking.

Bibles also come in the form of study Bibles which sprinkle interesting comments and study notes among its pages. Also interesting is the *Amplified Bible* which often uses several English words to describe each Greek or Hebrew word so that we get a fuller understanding of its meaning. However, that is what we will do ourselves as we dig into the original language.

As we look at each particular word, there is nothing like finding out which Greek or Hebrew word is being used. This is where chapters 6 and 7 come in. As I mentioned in those chapters, we don't have to know those languages to look up the meanings of the original words—there are some easy ways to do this. One way is to use an interlinear Bible. This shows the English word underneath each Greek or Hebrew word, and then we can use a Greek or Hebrew lexicon to look up its meaning. To make this even easier, some interlinear Bibles also supply a number for each Greek or Hebrew word—numbers that are also used in Strong's concordances and lexicons—making it easy to find the word. But easier yet, there is computer software that does all this for you! You can click on any English word and instantly look up the meaning of its Greek or Hebrew counterpart. *Bible Works* and *Logos Bible Software* are two excellent software packages you can buy and install on your computer. Each has many translations in English and other languages and can also take you to the Greek and Hebrew. Or, on the Internet you can go to the *Bible Gateway*, www.biblegateway.com, to do word searches and browse various translations for free.

Once I look up the Greek or Hebrew for each word and also look at several English translations, I often make my own "amplified" version of the text by putting square brackets after each word and adding the additional meaning I got from looking up the words. For example:

Do not marvel [be surprised, be amazed, be astonished] *that* [because] *I said to you* [singular], *"You* [plural] *must be born again* [anew, from above]." (John 3:7, NKJV)

Sometimes we may wish to get a better feel for a word by seeing how it is used elsewhere in the Bible. To do this there are concordances which list each word and the places where it is used. ("Complete" concordances list all the words and all the places where they are used.) There are English concordances, which do this for the English words (therefore they are dependent on the English translation used) and also Greek and Hebrew concordances. Again, the Bible software packages do this quickly and easily.

One of the most useful tools I have found is *Vine's* expository dictionary (or *Mounce's* dictionary, which is similar). Here you look up a word in English, and it tells you all the Greek words (plus their meanings) that represent that word. Sometimes it is very interesting to see that one Greek word was chosen over another in a given verse.

In the bibliography I provide the complete references to the resources I mention in this chapter.

Example: A New Creation

Therefore, if anyone is in Christ, he is a new creation.
(2 Corinthians 5:17, NIV)

First let's look at this same verse in several other translations.

- *Therefore if any man be in Christ, he is a new creature.* (KJV)

- *This means that anyone who belongs to Christ has become a new person.* (New Living Translation)

- *Now we look inside, and what we see is that anyone united with the Messiah gets a fresh start, is created new.* (The Message)

- Interlinear Greek and English:

  ὥστε εἴ τις ἐν Χριστῷ, καινὴ κτίσις·
  Therefore if anyone [is] in   Christ [he is] a new   creation.

Most of the words in this verse are straightforward to translate (which is why the literal translations are mostly the same for this verse). The only words to look up are those for "new" and "creation." The latter simply means the same as the English word and *Vine's* does not show us much here. However, for the word "new," *Vine's* gives us a gold mine. There are two words that could have been used: *kainos* and *neos*. *Neos* (which is not used) signifies new in respect of time: that which is recent. However, *kainos* (which is used) signifies new in respect to form or quality. If someone had a bicycle and got a new one, that would be a *neos* bicycle. However, if they invented a jet-propelled bicycle that could fly, that would be a *kainos* bicycle—a new type that no one had ever seen before. That is the kind of creation we have become: not just a renewed version of what we were, but made an entirely new type.

IV. IMMEDIATE CONTEXT

The verses before and after a verse often shed light onto what our verse is about. Even when those verses seem independent at first glance, the connections and comparisons between them might give us a lot of additional insight. Therefore, it often pays to give some thought to the question, "Why are these verses side by side?" Sometimes there is no reason. Sometimes it is because they are historical accounts which happened in that order. But even if the latter is true, God is the author of human history, and he could be trying to tell us something in their connections.

Example: The Story of Zacchaeus

> *Jesus entered Jericho and was passing through. A man was there by the name of Zacchaeus; he was a chief tax collector and was wealthy. . . . Jesus said to him, "Today salvation has come to this house, because this man, too, is a son of Abraham. For the Son of Man came to seek and to save what was lost."*
> (Luke 19:1–2, 9–10, NIV)

Realize first of all that, in that day, if a tax collector was rich, more than likely it was because he was cheating people. Also, being a son of Abraham, he was probably thought of as a turncoat, aiding the oppressive Roman regime. However, here was a man who became saved!

Looking at the surrounding verses, we find Luke 18:24–25 where Jesus said,

> *"How hard it is for the rich to enter the kingdom of God! Indeed, it is easier for a camel to go through the eye of a needle than for a rich man to enter the kingdom of God."*

This is quite interesting, since in the account of Zacchaeus, not only had a rich man entered the Kingdom of God, but he had become rich through dishonest means! And also interesting was that, in one of the earlier stories in Luke 18, the rich young ruler *had* kept the law but had not entered into the Kingdom of God.

It is no coincidence these two passages are side by side. For in one, the rich young ruler tried to gain salvation by the law and, in the other, Zacchaeus had probably given up trying to gain anything by being good, but grace came his way. In fact, the five accounts before that of Zacchaeus are all about how and how not to be saved. Luke 18:9–14 talks of a self-righteous Pharisee in contrast with a tax collector saying "Have mercy on me, a sinner." The tax collector walked away justified by God; the Pharisee did not. In Luke 18:15–17 Jesus says we have to receive the Kingdom like a little child. Luke 18:18–30 is the story of the rich young ruler. In Luke 18:31–34 the dismayed disciples asked Jesus who can be saved, at which point he "comforts" them by telling them of his upcoming death. And in Luke 18:35–43 a blind beggar asks for mercy and receives it. So we see that salvation comes through repentance, from an attitude like a child, from the price Jesus paid, and by receiving grace and mercy. It does not come from self-righteousness or the law. Hence the connection of these verses itself tells a story that we might miss if we only looked at the verses standing on their own.

V. ISSUES

By now you may realize that, as you go through these steps praying that God would illuminate his Word, the spiritual truths will come pouring in. Write them all down. We will discuss choosing the theme of your talk and trimming and organizing all your thoughts later.

Example: Jesus Changes Water into Wine

On the third day a wedding took place at Cana in Galilee. Jesus' mother was there, and Jesus and his disciples had also been invited to the wedding. When the wine was gone, Jesus' mother said to him, "They have no more wine." "Dear woman, why do you involve me?" Jesus replied, "My time has not yet come." His mother said to the servants, "Do whatever he tells you." Nearby stood six stone water jars, the kind used by the Jews for ceremonial washing, each holding from twenty to thirty gallons. Jesus said to the servants, "Fill the jars with water"; so they filled them to the brim. Then he told them, "Now draw some out and take it to the master of the banquet." They did so, and the master of the banquet tasted the water that had been turned into wine. He did not realize where it had come from, though the servants who had drawn the water knew. Then he called the bridegroom aside and said, "Everyone brings out the choice wine first and then the cheaper wine after the guests have had too much to drink; but you have saved the best till now." This, the first of his miraculous signs, Jesus performed in Cana of Galilee. He thus revealed his glory, and his disciples put their faith in him. (John 2:1–11)

Here are some thoughts that may come from a cursory reading of this text:

- Jesus honored his mother, who also honored him.
- The water jars were used for ceremonial washings to make people "clean."
- Each jar held twenty to thirty gallons, so this miracle produced a lot of wine!

- Jesus' mother and the servants carried out a simple act of obedience in filling the jars with water, an obedience which led to the miracle.
- The excellent wine showed the touch of God, who does everything well.
- The fact that it was called a "sign" shows it was pointing to something.
- If God could transform water to wine, he could transform our souls into something new.
- This wrought faith in the disciples.

There are probably many more points we could make, especially when going through all the steps. At this time, don't be concerned about whether your points all fit or what order they are in. We will get to that later.

VI. CENTRAL THOUGHT

By this time you have probably encountered many truths the text is revealing. Now you should be identifying the central thought of the text. Ask yourself: what is the author's passion for writing the text? This helps in determining what it is you want to convey. It may be, however, that in this teaching session God wants you to focus on one of the subthemes of the text. So the important question is: what is the central thought God wants to convey to your hearers today?

Example: Jesus Changes Water into Wine (John 2:1–11)

Of all the issues we listed for this text, what will be our central thought? Again, that will depend on what God wants to say to our hearers. In thinking about the passion Jesus had in doing what he did, it probably was not centered around producing good wine (although he may have enjoyed seeing the people blessed at the wedding). His main passion was to show his disciples who he was and to instill faith in him as he began his ministry, in which he would be transforming far more than jars of water. So we might want to choose how Jesus transforms people as our central thought. (But if we taught on this again in a few months, maybe we would choose a different central thought.)

VII. RELATED TEXTS

Once we know the thought we are centering upon, we may want to find other texts that support or expand upon our points.

Example: David's Last Psalm

The LORD has dealt with me according to my righteousness; according to the cleanness of my hands he has rewarded me. For I have kept the ways of the LORD; I have not done evil by turning from my God. All his laws are before me; I have not turned away from his decrees. I have been blameless before him and have kept myself from sin. The LORD has rewarded me according to my righteousness, according to my cleanness in his sight. (2 Samuel 22:21–25)

As one reads this, he or she may think: "Wait a minute, David, how can you be talking about how clean and righteous you were? Don't you remember what happened with Bathsheba?" When you get a thought like that, don't try to gloss over it. God may be leading you to dig into something deeper. Maybe you should even make this thought front and center! So in this text, how could David say what he did? The last sentence gives us the key: "according to my cleanness *in his sight* [emphasis mine]." This is what is amazing about forgiveness: when God forgives, he truly forgets and, in his sight, it is no more. Therefore a good related text to use is this one:

I, even I, am he who blots out your transgressions, for my own sake, and remembers your sins no more. (Isaiah 43:25)

How amazing is that? David, in his old age, had learned how to see himself through God's eyes and could truly see himself as clean and righteous. So can we.

VIII. ILLUSTRATIONS

In chapter 2 I discussed how often the Bible uses illustrations to make its points. They capture our attention, enhance our ability to learn, and stay in our memories a long time. So in teaching, it is always good to think of illustrations to go with the points we are trying to make. Those illustrations can come from our own experiences (which is an excellent way to connect with our hearers) or the experiences of others. Illustrations can also be drawn from history or from Scripture itself.

Example: Racham

As a father has compassion on [KJV: pities] *his children, so the LORD has compassion on those who fear him.* (Psalm 103:13)

The word "has compassion on" (also translated as "pities") is an odd choice of words for how we feel toward our children. Would you say you *pitied* your children? The Hebrew word is *racham*. About thirty years ago I heard an Old Testament professor talk about this verse. He gave an illustration about the word *racham* that I have never forgotten. He told us that this word could only be properly explained through a story. He said to imagine ourselves with one of our children at a county fair. Somehow that child wanders away and we frantically begin searching for him. The search goes to ten minutes, then twenty. Suddenly we see our child across the way and, as we run toward each other, we embrace and feel his little chest press against ours. That feeling beating in our heart right now is *racham*. As a father *rachams* his children, so the Lord *rachams* us.

IX. APPLICATION

David Mains has spent his life teaching pastors how to give effective sermons. For a sermon not to end up in the "black hole" of forgetfulness, he says that we need to make sure that people can easily tell you (1) what your sermon was about, (2) what they should do about it, and (3) when they should do it. As we are preparing a teaching, it is imperative to ask ourselves: what are we asking the hearer to do? (Granted, some teachings are just to impart knowledge, and that is fine once in a while. But in the long run, we do not just want people to be filled with knowledge—we also want people to be *changed* and to be change-agents in the world.) Therefore, as you prepare to teach, ask God, "What are you asking the people to do in response to this word?"

Somewhat connected to this step is asking what God might want to do for the people during a ministry time after the message. Praying for people like this brings an impartation from God in ways that can be personal and powerful.

Example: Dissension among Brothers

> *There are six things the* LORD *hates, seven that are detestable to him: haughty eyes, a lying tongue, hands that shed innocent blood, a heart that devises wicked schemes, feet that are quick to rush into evil, a false witness who pours out lies and a man who stirs up dissension among brothers.* (Proverbs 6:16–19)

Here is a rather negative text that I have used when warning about creating dissension and disunity. (It is interesting that the Lord finds that more detestable than the other six things he hates!) Even though I teach about the dangers of disunity directly, in order to apply such a teaching, I don't ask that the hearers merely store away this information. I usually don't even ask them to make a promise to change (although that is not a bad idea). The way I usually apply it is to paint a picture of the opposite situation and ask them to try that. Here, I ask them to imagine what it would be like if, instead of sowing discord, we gave sincere encouragement to one another. I point out the times I have received such encouragement (either by relaying something a person felt the Lord was saying to me or by expressing their own heartfelt appreciation) and describe how I have been energized to go a mile on it. (The one speaking always receives a feeling of satisfaction as well.) If, instead of cutting each other down, we were to often do this, imagine what our church would be like! So during my teaching, I might give them opportunity to encourage one another right then or have them do it during the week and see what happens.

X. COMMENTARIES

I put the use of commentaries late in the process of digging into a text so that you will not lean on others to do the digging for you. In comparing commentaries, you will often find that one has insights another did not have and vice versa. In other words, commentaries are not the end-all when it comes to insights—you may well discover some on your own (with God's help) that others have not mentioned. So dig into the text and look for insights yourself first. Then you can read the insights of someone else to see what you may have missed.

One of the more useful things I find in commentaries are historical insights that are pertinent to the text. One book that focuses on this is *The New Manners and Customs of the Bible*.

You never know in which commentary (or book) you may run across a really good insight, so when you find one that is a gem, jot it down (plus its reference). Having a file full of such insights will prove invaluable.

Example: The Prodigal Son

> Jesus continued: "There was a man who had two sons. The younger one said to his father, 'Father, give me my share of the estate.' So he divided his property between them. Not long after that, the younger son got together all he had, set off for a distant country and there squandered his wealth in wild living. . . . So he got up and went to his father. But while he was still a long way off, his father saw him and was filled with compassion for him; he ran to his son, threw his arms around him and kissed him. . . . " (Luke 15:11–24)

One of the best commentaries that helped me with this text came in the person of one of my seminary professors who knew a lot about the culture of Jesus' day. He said that when the son asked his father for his share of the estate, that was tantamount to saying to him, "I wish you were dead." That gives a little more insight into why the son would have been reluctant to come home and why his only hope was to be hired as a servant. Another thing this professor said was that, in that culture, it was extremely uncouth for a grown man to run. The father obviously did not care what anyone thought, but ran to his son out of unabashed love for him—in order to experience that *racham* I talked about before.

XI. ORGANIZE

Now that you have many thoughts about your text (as well as having a central thought), it is time to trim and organize. Ask yourself: what will impact the listeners the most?

As you speak, make sure your hearers always know what the subject is that you are talking about. Someone once said, "Tell them what you are going to say, say it, then tell them what you said." That keeps them from getting lost and also makes what you say memorable, maybe even to the point that they can teach it to others.

What I usually do is look at all my thoughts and think of three to five major points I want to make (assigning a Roman numeral to each). Then I go through all the thoughts I had jotted down and, for each one of them, write down the Roman numeral it should fall under. I also add numbers to each thought, indicating the order in which I will say it. Often quite a few of my thoughts will be trimmed out and put into my file to talk about another time. Remember: you don't have to say everything that comes to your mind—just say enough to impact the hearers. It is better to leave them inspired and hungry to learn more rather than to leave them overloaded.

It is also important to think how you will begin and end your talk. The beginning is when you have the greatest amount of everyone's attention, and your introduction will determine how much of their attention they will continue to give you. The end of the talk is usually the part people remember best, so it is good to review the points you made in a way that has as much impact as possible.

Example: God and Music

Do not get drunk on wine, which leads to debauchery. Instead, be filled with the Spirit. Speak to one another with psalms, hymns and spiritual songs. Sing and make music in your heart to the Lord. (Ephesians 5:18–19)

Here I was teaching on worship, specifically asking what it is about music that seems so special to God. In my notes for this talk, I looked up every Biblical reference to music. Obviously I had a lot to trim and organize. I decided to talk about these major points:

I. Introduction
II. The Supernatural Aspect of Music
III. The Call of Worship on Our Hearts
IV. Dimensions of Worship
V. Conclusion

So I assigned each of my notes to one of these categories and prayed how to best say each one. For the introduction, I read the text and said I was going to explore the connection between walking in the Spirit and music, asking the people: "What is so special about music, anyway, especially to God?" (I made it like a mystery, and they seemed to want to keep tuned in to find the answer.) In the introduction I also did a demonstration from my days teaching physics showing how vibrating strings produce musical sounds, throwing in some asides of how harmony works in music and its similarity to being in harmony with one other. That added to the mystery of how something so natural could have a spiritual connection.

In my middle three points, I talked about how Elisha and David used music to prophesy and bring sanity and how important Jesus said that worship was. I also spoke of how there are remarkable dimensions in worship (such as liberating praise versus deep worship), some of which we have just begun to explore. As an application, I invited the hearers to explore these dimensions as they worshiped at home. I also gave examples of how music seems to have an effect on human beings and that God seems to have made us that way.

As a conclusion I decided to use an illustration that would unveil a side of me not many knew—my background in particle physics. I knew people would either find that very interesting or I would lose them. Fortunately, the former turned out to be the case. I reviewed the quest of science to find the fundamental building blocks of the universe. Early on, those building blocks seemed to be elements, but elements were later found to be made up of protons and neutrons. Recently, however, protons and neutrons were found to be made up of particles called *quarks*. Now theorists are looking at even more fundamental building blocks than these: *strings*. These are strings of energy undergoing various modes of vibrations into ten different dimensions (seven more than we know about). The different ways these strings vibrate correspond to the different known particles. I then gave this quote from Michio Kaku, Professor of Theoretical Physics at CUNY:

> "Just as a violin string's different vibrations produce different notes, energy strings' unique vibration patterns correspond to different subatomic particles. If this picture is correct, all of physics can be summarized as the harmonies of tiny vibrating strings, chemistry as the melodies of interacting strings, and the universe as a symphony of all strings resonating distinctly."

Suddenly, in the quest for the building blocks of the universe, there appears . . . music! Maybe music is far more special to God than we ever imagined. My concluding sentences reviewed the main thought as well as what I was asking of the people: "There are many things in the world and in the heavens with which we can resonate—some good, some bad. Let our lives be ones that resonate with worship unto the Lord. That's what he had in mind when he made us."

XII. PRAY

Before we give our teaching, we need to go before the Lord and ask, "God, what do you want to say to the people?" Those people are precious to him and there is always something burning on his heart that he wants to say to them. We need to capture that passion so we can say it in the way he would say it. I'm constantly looking for that passion before, during, and after I go through all this preparation.

Ask the Holy Spirit to be with you as you prepare and as you speak. His presence with you can give you his passion. His presence on you and on those who hear your words will bring his work into their hearts as his words are spoken. There really is no substitute for the empowering and anointing of the Holy Spirit.

Example: The Restoration of Peter

"I tell you the truth, when you were younger you dressed yourself and went where you wanted; but when you are old you will stretch out your hands, and someone else will dress you and lead you where you do not want to go." Jesus said this to indicate the kind of death by which Peter would glorify God. Then he said to him, "Follow me!" (John 21:18–19)

As Jesus was restoring Peter, who had been crushed after realizing he had been so weak as to deny Jesus three times, Jesus said one of the shockingly unusual things he was prone to say: he told Peter how he would die for him. You would think that during Peter's restoration he might say something a little more comforting! However, remember that in Mark 14:27–31 Peter had said he would die for Jesus, but now it had become clear he could not even live for him. So in his masterful restoration, Jesus first reinstated Peter's call. Then, as the ultimate piece, he showed Peter that he really would give his life for Jesus' cause. That is what Peter needed to hear. It must have changed Peter because in Acts 2 he was first to speak at Pentecost, in Acts 4 he boldly spoke before the Sanhedrin, and at the end of his life was crucified like Jesus. And in his letters he gave such powerful advice to those undergoing persecution that scholars have dubbed him the "Apostle to the Persecuted."

In praying for this message I asked, "God, what is on your heart for the people?" What I felt God say to me is that, so often, the people feel like failures. They started out with dreams from him but couldn't even seem to get past the little things in life, so their dreams simply seemed impossible. God, who restored Peter, also wants to restore these people and let them have their dreams again. It may not be a dream of dying for Jesus, but whatever dream he has given them, he wants it—and them—restored.

Thinking More About It

Ω There is nothing like doing one yourself! Pick one of your favorite verses and go through the twelve steps. Did any step show you something you hadn't thought about before?

CHAPTER TEN

HOW TO TEACH THE WORD

In the previous chapter I described how to do a teaching based upon one verse. That is called a textual Bible study. Sometimes you may want to teach on a subject and, in so doing, use several different verses. This is called a topical Bible study. There are many ways of doing this. Sometimes the topic lends itself to how you will teach it. Other times it is what you feel is best for you and your hearers. In this chapter I will discuss several different ways you might teach on a topic which, I hope, will ignite your creativity as you partner with God in teaching what is on his heart and yours.

CLUSTER OF TEXTS

In the last chapter, which focused on teaching a particular verse, I encouraged you to find supporting verses. It often happens that one or more of these supporting verses receives almost as much attention as the first.

Example: The Pearl of Great Price

Again, the kingdom of heaven is like a merchant looking for fine pearls. When he found one of great value, he went away and sold everything he had and bought it. (Matthew 13:45–46)

In researching this verse I found that there were differences of opinion as to what the pearl represented. The traditional view is that the pearl represents the Kingdom and we represent the merchant selling all we have to buy it. But another view is that God is the merchant and we are the pearl—God certainly paid quite a price to buy us. Rather than gloss over the differences in these views, I did a teaching which highlighted them.

I first made a good case for the traditional view (the verses preceding this parable give this support), using my own life as an example of how much I was willing to sell all for what God had to offer. Then I introduced the other view. Here I picked up on the pearl being something that was found and turned to Luke 15 where there are three other parables about things that were found: a lost sheep, a lost coin, and a lost son. I spent a great deal of time on the latter—the story of the prodigal son. Finally, at the end of that discussion, I went back to the pearl of great price. In the story of the prodigal son, the thing that was found was the son and the finder was the father. This led to the supposition that, in the story of the pearl of great price, the finder of the pearl may also be the Father—therefore the pearl of such great price is you and me. It is a stunning realization that God finds us of such value. But he really does. That is, in fact, what the story of the prodigal son is all about.

So, having made a good case for each point of view, I had to answer the question: which is the right one? Actually, the text itself doesn't rule out either. It only says that the Kingdom of God is about finding treasure—things of great value. And there is more than one treasure to be found. God is our treasure; we are his.

The coming of the Kingdom is about opening eyes to show people what a treasure God is to them, but also what a treasure they are to God—both are staggering and life-changing realizations. Such is the nature of the Kingdom: we find pearls of great price and so does God.

LIVING OUT A NARRATIVE

Sometimes, rather than teach on a single verse, it is interesting to go through an entire narrative in Scripture. Here you can encourage the people to imagine they are in the story and let them feel what those people must have felt. The narrative was given to grasp and change our hearts, so we can pretty much let the narrative teach itself.

Example: The Story of Gideon

Judges 6–7 tells the wonderful story of a man, Gideon, who was reluctant to be used by God but was powerfully used anyway. In teaching on this, I found it very effective to insert a little bit of commentary and let the story speak for itself.

First, in a brief introduction, I asked the people to keep a close watch on Gideon and see what turned him into a "mighty man of valor."

The background to the story is actually given in the text itself (Judges 6:1–10), so all that was necessary was to read it.

Starting in verse 11, we see a conversation between Gideon and the angel of the Lord. In verse 13, I pointed out that Gideon longed for the days of God moving in power, which God wants us to long for as well. As I read through Gideon's interactions with the Lord, I highlighted how contrary he seemed to be to a "mighty man of valor." He started out by hiding in a winepress (v. 11). He felt he was the weakest member of the weakest clan (v. 15). In realizing whom he was speaking to, he thought he was going to die (vv. 22–23). He was obedient to tear down the altar to Baal, but did it at night so as not to be seen (v. 27). Because he doubted he was hearing right, he set out not one, but two fleeces before the Lord (vv. 36–40).

In verse 34 something began to happen, however. "The Spirit of the Lord came upon Gideon," and Gideon became a leader.

Judges 7 then describes the battle Gideon led. First God instructed him to cut down the number of warriors: from thirty-two thousand to ten thousand and then to three hundred (vv. 1–8). Large numbers obviously do not impress God. The strategy of warfare that God had Gideon use is fascinating. Actually, the same strategy can be used by the enemy against us (the strategies of warfare can be used by anyone), so it is instructive to see how it works. First, God sowed doubt in the enemy (vv. 9–15). (We, too, can sow a good "doubt" in people yet to know the Lord, that the way they look at life may be lacking.) Then God sowed fear, confusion, a lack of communication, and division in the enemy (vv. 16–22a). (Think how many times the enemy has tried that same strategy on us.) Finally, God caused the enemy to choose retreat (vv. 22b–25). This sealed their defeat, and the battle was won. God had used Gideon mightily.

A good conclusion to this narrative can be drawn from two verses found in Judges 8:

> *The Israelites said to Gideon, "Rule over us—"... But Gideon told them, "I will not rule over you, nor will my son rule over you. The LORD will rule over you!"* (Judges 8:22–23)

So maybe this is why Gideon was chosen: he was humble and obedient and, above all, realized God was his strength. We see in the end that he learned this lesson well. We, too, need to have the humility and willingness to listen, rise up in the faith of Gideon, let the Spirit come on us, and go for it.

CONNECTION BETWEEN TWO THEMES

Oftentimes we can focus on a theme of the Bible, collect verses about it, and teach on it. Sometimes it is interesting to look at two themes and the interaction between them. This is particularly instructive for some of the themes we looked at in our survey of systematic theology.

For instance, we could look at the law individually or at grace individually. However, when you look at them together, you learn a lot more about both and when to use one as opposed to the other.

Example: God's Righteousness and Mercy

This was covered in chapter 8, so I won't cover it again other than to say both righteousness and mercy are attributes of God. Looking at the extent of how fallen we were, these two attributes were in tension, with our very lives in the balance. Nowhere was this tension more strongly felt than in the heart of God. As is often the case when themes seem to come into conflict, something great can be seen when looking at them together. This particular conflict gave rise to the greatest plan of all time, a plan which was conceived by the greatest heart in the universe, a plan where "mercy and truth have met together; righteousness and peace have kissed." (Psalm 85:10, NKJV) The plan, of course, involved the sacrifice of Jesus. It was a plan that cost God everything. There was no solution to our dilemma other than this.

SURVEY OF AN ENTIRE BOOK

Looking at an entire book of the Bible can instill a love for that book and empower us to read it with more interest and understanding. If you ever find yourself teaching your way through a book of the Bible, a survey is a great way to begin.

Example: The Book of John—Jesus the "Greater Than"

Throughout his book, John's words are very simple yet very deep. John was overwhelmed with who Jesus truly was and the fact that he knew him (1 John 1:1). John 20:31 says the purpose of the book is this: "But these are written that you may believe that Jesus is the Christ, the Son of God, and that by believing you may have life in his name." From the beginning, John looks at Jesus as God and as the one who took on the role as the Lamb of God, and this is the way to have life in his name.

The book of John is a good way to introduce people to the Hebrew teaching style. This style not only uses many illustrations (as I discussed in chapter 2), but it is often repetitive and cyclical. That is, in order to effectively teach, the teacher often repeats things, sometimes cycling through these repetitions, each with a slightly different perspective. John, wanting us to know how Jesus truly was God, cycled through Jesus being "I Am" seven different times:

- *I am the bread of life.* (John 6:35)
- *I am the light of the world.* (John 8:12)
- *I am the gate for the sheep.* (John 10:7)
- *I am the good shepherd.* (John 10:14)
- *I am the resurrection and the life.* (John 11:25)
- *I am the way and the truth and the life.* (John 14:6)
- *I am the true vine.* (John 15:1)

Jesus also attested that "before Abraham was born, I am!" (v. 8:58) and, when the soldiers went to arrest him, they fell over backward at the power of his saying "I am He." (vv. 18:5–6, NKJV).

There are also seven major miracles in John (2:1–11; 4:46–54; 5:1–15; 6:1–15; 6:16–21; 9:1–34; 11:1–44), which is fascinating because they were similar to miracles in the Old Testament, but usually greater. John 1:17 says, "For the law was given through Moses; grace and truth came through Jesus Christ." The miracles, then, attest to Jesus being the "Greater Than"—greater than the law or the prophets. For example, Moses turned the bitter water sweet (Exodus 15:22–25), but Jesus turned water into wine (John 2:1–11). Elisha fed one hundred men from twenty loaves (2 Kings 4:42–44), Jesus fed five thousand from five loaves (John 6:1–15). Moses parted the water (Exodus 14:21–22), Jesus walked on top of it (John 6:16–21).

The amazement of John realizing who Jesus was is never more evident than in the prologue (John 1:1–13) where John shows Jesus being with God in the beginning, taking part in creation, and now being sent for our "re-creation." After portraying Jesus in this majesty, John then states, "The Word became flesh and made his dwelling among us." (John 1:14) That is, after looking at his heavenly majesty, John points us to the most amazing thing that had happened—he had become one of us. And now John begins to describe in the rest of his book what this Son of God was like.

WORD STUDY

A good way to teach on a theme is by showing how a word is used throughout the Bible or throughout one of its books. In *The Presence, Power and Heart of God*, I did this with the word "amazed" in the book of Mark in order to see how the disciples' worldviews had changed as they spent time with Jesus. Even if it is not for a teaching, it is often very instructive to do this on your own. (A word search using Bible software is very easy to do.)

Example: The Words "River" and "Lake" Used in the Bible

I became interested in this when reading *The Other Side of Pastoral Ministry* by a pastor named Daniel Brown, who said there are two ways to look at a church. We can look at it like a lake, where we gauge success by numbers, or we can look at it like a river, where we gauge success by how far its people move down the river of their spiritual growth. He clearly was promoting the river model, with which I heartily agree.

One day a question came to me whether God might prefer rivers over lakes (or vice versa) in the Bible—not real rivers and lakes, of course, but instances where the words are used symbolically. I found that God is *very* opinionated about this!

First of all, what is the difference between rivers and lakes when they are used symbolically? Simply put, in rivers water moves, and in lakes it doesn't. So a river would symbolize something that is flowing, moving, or changing. A lake would symbolize something that is standing still.

I began by looking at the references to rivers. In two of those references, Isaiah 43:2 and Luke 6:48, a river depicts the flow of everyday life, which can sweep over a person. Often we try to make our lives into a lake, trying to keep everything standing still, only to discover it really is a river with its swells that can sweep over us and its bends where people can become stuck.

Most of the references for river, however, depict the river of God: the Holy Spirit (John 7:38–39) or God's attributes (Psalm 36:8, Isaiah 48:18, Amos 5:24). These rivers are a fresh unfolding of his goodness, changing us and taking us somewhere.

The only references to lake were found in Revelation (19:20; 20:10,14,15; 21:8) which referred to the lake of fire: constant, never-ending turmoil. Definitely not a positive connotation!

Two of the most interesting references to a river I left to the end. One is Ezekiel 47:1–12, the river flowing from the temple of God. It starts ankle-deep and becomes deep enough to swim in. Life grows in it and along its shore. What I never saw before this word study, however, was in verse 11: "But the swamps and marshes will not become fresh; they will be left for salt." Why is this? It is because their water is not moving! It is not refreshed by the moving river of God.

The last reference is equally as interesting. It is found in the last chapter of the Bible, Revelation 22:1–2, where heaven is being portrayed. And what is there in heaven? A river! "Then the angel showed me the river of the water of life, as clear as crystal, flowing from the throne of God and of the Lamb. . . . On each side of the river stood the tree of life. . . . And the leaves of the tree are for the healing of the nations." So even heaven will not be stagnant, but a continual unfolding of God's goodness!

In praying how to apply this, the Lord took me back to the river of everyday life, with people often stuck in its bends when that river had taken unexpected turns. What is important to remember is that there are two rivers talked about in Scripture: the river of everyday life and the river of God. If we can get into the river of God, it can help us be freed from those bends where we are stuck in life. Life is a river, and we may just as well get used to it. But rather than just being pushed around by that river, God invites us to jump into *his* river and be taken on the adventure of our lives, always changing, constantly taking us to the spiritual places where he would have us be next.

SMALL GROUP INTERACTIVE APPROACH

Research into effective teaching has shown there are some methods which are the best ways for students to learn and be changed. Some I have mentioned already: repetition and illustration. Perhaps the most effective method, however, is to get the students involved in the learning process by interacting and even teaching the material themselves. Soliciting interaction, therefore, is invaluable. It is perfect in small group settings. It is so valuable, in fact, that I occasionally try to get some interaction going in large group situations as well.

In small group settings it is usually not too difficult to come up with questions that elicit discussion. There is also material, such as the *Serendipity New Testament for Groups*, that contains sample questions for every section of Scripture, which a small group might want to study.

There are some general questions you can ask the people in your group: how did they feel in reading the text, what was the central thought, and what experiences have they had that illustrate this thought? You can also ask how that truth has impacted their lives and what they plan to do about what they have just discussed. Let the discussion go in interesting directions, but be ready to sum up the central point at the end, trying to end in a way that impacts people's lives.

Example: John 3

> *Jesus declared, "I tell you the truth, no one can see the Kingdom of God unless he is born again.". . . "Just as Moses lifted up the snake in the desert, so the Son of Man must be lifted up. . . . For God so loved the world that he gave his one and only Son."* (John 3:3,14a,16)

This is a good text for asking how people felt in reading it. Like Nicodemus, they may find the words "born again" a bit odd. They may find Jesus being compared to a snake even more shocking. (Numbers 21:4–9 gives the background to that reference.) At some point you can bring in 2 Corinthians 5:21, saying how Jesus became sin, and how that is just as shocking as comparing Jesus to the snake. Then looking at 1 John 1:5, which says that no darkness can be in God, you can ask what must have happened with the fellowship between Jesus and God when Jesus became sin on the cross. That should add even more punch when you get to John 3:16, seeing how hard it must have been for God to send his only Son and how much he must have loved us to do that.

Asking how this has impacted (and continues to impact) people's lives should bring out interesting discussions. You could even end by asking, "If you were the only person in the world, would God have sent his Son for you?"

Thinking More About It

Ω Think of a topic and come up with a creative idea on how to present it.

CHAPTER ELEVEN

HOW TO APPLY AND ENJOY THE WORD

The Word was given so that we may know God—both know about him and know him personally. But it is also imminently practical in how it affects our lives and, in turn, affects others through our lives. It is also given for our sheer enjoyment—an enjoyment of the Word itself and an enjoyment of God to whom the Word can bring us close.

PRACTICAL THEOLOGY

Seminaries offer a number of courses on practical theology, from evangelism to marriage and family counseling to drug and alcohol intervention. There are similar topics, for which courses are rarely offered (but should be), from ministry to the poor to intercession to various kinds of healing. There are hundreds of books written on each one of these topics and I won't try to go into them here. But I do want to say that as we relate to, counsel, and pray for people in various situations in life, we get to know the sort of things people are going through. And we also get to know the amazing way the Lord can and does help people in need. Engaging in these activities makes our teaching more compassionate, relevant, applicable, and powerful.

THE PASSION OF THE CHRIST

In becoming equipped to teach the Word, we can learn all sorts of knowledge, how to do research, how to effectively organize what we are going to say, how to say it, and how to make it applicable to others' lives. All of this is important—even vital. But it will fall short of what it could be unless we present it with the heart of the Lord.

In writing this book, I have had an unusual, increasing desire to know the passion of Jesus: what was that inner fire in him as he spoke? What did he want the people to know and do? I have always wanted to have a passion *for* Jesus, but recently I've had an increasing desire to know the passion *of* Jesus. It's a desire that I expect will be a never-ending pursuit. The title of this section: "The Passion of the Christ" is, of course, a play on words regarding Mel Gibson's movie about the suffering and death of Jesus on the cross. The passion of Jesus I'm describing here is what was inside his heart that drove him to say what he said and do what he did. Yet this is also the very same passion that drove him to his suffering and death. So what is this passion of the Christ?

As I thought about this, I remembered the first sermon I ever gave after I had entered seminary. It was on the shortest verse in the Bible: John 11:35, "Jesus wept." At the time I may have chosen that text because I thought I could handle a verse that short. It turned out to be a difficult verse, however, because most the commentators differed as to why they thought Jesus wept. This intrigued me, though, because when you see someone expressing emotion, you are often close to knowing their inner feelings. And Scripture only records two instances of Jesus weeping: here and in Luke 19:41 when he wept over Jerusalem.

So why did Jesus weep? I can think of three things that may have made this happen, perhaps all being felt by Jesus simultaneously. First, the circumstance may have been like that of Luke 19:41, which shows Jesus weeping over Jerusalem out of sorrow, but also with a little frustration—God the Son was standing in front of Jerusalem desirous to gather them as a hen gathers her chicks under her wings, and it did not recognize the time of God's coming. Similarly in John 11:35, among the loud mourning over death, the Resurrection and the Life was standing in front of them, and they did not recognize it. Second, the weeping of Mary over the loss of her brother was deeply moving to Jesus. Scripture tells us to "weep with those who weep" (Romans 12:15, NKJV) and Jesus, who exemplified every aspect of love, would have done this as well. It is interesting that, as we are trying to put ourselves in Jesus' shoes to feel what he felt, we find him doing the very thing with Mary, feeling her ache due to the pain of death. Third, as Jesus "wept with those who wept," maybe he was also weeping with the Father. Looking at the nature of God, we see that God certainly feels emotions. It was the pain of eternal death and his deep love for those who were heading in that direction that was the reason why God sent his only Son. Jesus carried around the heart of the Father, so seeing the pain of physical death would have had to remind him of the pain of eternal death that was so much on his Father's heart. Maybe Jesus' human heart could not contain this emotion. All three of these reasons can be summarized as Jesus weeping over the pain of a broken world: a world that was being besieged with physical death, facing eternal death, and not recognizing the time of God's coming to it.

> **When Jesus spoke to the multitudes, what was his passion and underlying desire?**

So when Jesus spoke to the multitudes, what was his passion and underlying desire? What must he have been like when he spoke? People would come in droves and sit all day, often with nothing to eat, just to hear him talk. They couldn't stay away! He spoke words of truth and life. There was life in his eyes, and they knew his authority was different than anything they had ever known. They could feel his heartfelt passion for their well-being—how much he loved them. He wanted them to know the beauty of the Kingdom he was there to offer. It pained him to see the trouble they were in—suffering in a broken world, strong-armed by the hand of the enemy, ultimately to be led off to their eternal death. He wanted to pull them from this into his Kingdom, where they would be safe and know true life, light, freedom, and truth. His desire for this to happen was so deep that it led him to the cross.

There are other aspects to Jesus' passion, as well. As odd as it sounds, having just discussed Jesus weeping, mixed in with his passion was also joy. To be sure, Jesus often spoke with intensity—he was both Lion and Lamb. But he also must have felt joy, since "in Your presence is fullness of joy" (Psalm 16:11, NKJV). Even in his suffering, joy was in his thoughts: "For the joy set before him [Jesus] endured the cross" (Hebrews 12:2). To love people, to see them coming into his Kingdom, to do what the Father was doing, to be *with* the Father . . . all of these gave Jesus—and gives us—a deep joy, the likes of which can be found nowhere else.

If we seek the passion of Jesus, we must also seek the presence of the Holy Spirit. That is what gave Peter passion, power, and effectiveness as he preached at Pentecost, resulting in three thousand people coming to the Lord. The Spirit was with Jesus when he spoke and ministered, and that same Spirit is willing to be with us as well. There is no comparison in what happens when the Holy Spirit is with us as we speak. Ask for Jesus' passion and for the Holy Spirit to come—he loves to answer those requests!

The more we seek it, the more we will grow in knowing the passion of Jesus. If we let it, it can also be *our* passion in what we do and say. As we read the Bible, we will find that every verse about Jesus manifests his heart in a slightly new and different way. These verses are just waiting for us to jump into, to wear his shoes for a while, and to feel what he felt. When we do that, we can teach what these verses are saying with his heart and passion—a passion that can penetrate people's hearts and draw them into his wonderful Kingdom.

ENJOYING THE WORD

In the past several chapters I have been talking about digging into the Word as if we were preparing to teach it. Most of the time, however, we read the Word simply to enjoy it. This is the way it should be. Out of those times have actually come the best ideas for teaching. But even if that were not to happen, just the joy of knowing the Lord through his Word is reward enough.

There are some ways to increase this joy. I had a New Testament professor who complained that some tried to put the Word into theological cellophane-wrapped packages, like meat displayed in a supermarket. Instead, we should let Jesus speak it to us the way he said it and enjoy each word like a juicy piece of steak, letting its juices swirl around our mouth as we savor its succulence. (My apologies to vegetarians for this analogy!)

Another way is not to worship the Bible itself (which almost always amounts to our worshipping our own understanding of it), but to seek and enjoy him who spoke it. The Word portrays itself as being given to know *him*. Yes, he will be totally congruous with his Word, but it is *he* who wants to pull us into his arms. Our Christianity must be more than a mental construct of information we have gathered or sermons we have heard. I once heard an illustration accredited to Søren Kierkegaard who pictured two doors in heaven: one labeled "Lectures about God," which had many waiting to go in, and another simply labeled "God," which had few in line. According to the parable of the prodigal son, I think the father would be a little disappointed if, after having redeemed his son, his son were to choose "lectures about the father" over the father himself. So do what he desires—come to him and enjoy his being with you.

Finally, since the Holy Spirit was given to lead us into all truth and to remind us of all that Jesus has said—and since he, the Father, and the Son are with us—make God part of your times in the Word. Ask him what it means when you are reading it—what he was feeling at the time. A friend of mine reads the Word like this and often says, "God, I've read this all my life and really don't know what it means. Help me with it." He has gotten some of the most mind-boggling insights that I have ever heard. Sometimes we expect the pastor to come up with insights but never expect to have them ourselves. Ask!

THE ADVENTURE OF OUR LIVES

It is an adventure we are on with God. He has given us so many things to help us in this life. And his Word is one of the most amazing of those things. In the Word we see many others who have been on this adventure with him, learning what he was trying to have them learn, failing at times, getting back up, and enjoying being with God in the process. May the Word speak life to you, and may his passion burn within you as you share God's words of life with your generation and the next.

APPENDIX

QUIZZES AND RESOURCES

Think of these as puzzles to enjoy. The answers follow at the end of this section on pages 145–146.

QUIZ ONE: THE BOOKS OF THE OLD TESTAMENT

Name the Old Testament book for each description below:

1. Perhaps the earliest written book in the Bible

2. The life of Elisha (successor to Elijah)

3. Written 100 years after the exile, said the Lord's day was coming but that Elijah would be sent first

4. The account of Moses as a baby floating in the Nile

5. A vision of Israel depicted as dry bones coming to life

6. The account of Jacob wrestling with an angel

7. The story of Samson and Delilah

8. The beauty of love between a king and his wife

9. An astounding prediction of how the Messiah would suffer and what that would mean

10. The second book of Jeremiah

QUIZ TWO: THE BOOKS OF THE NEW TESTAMENT

Name the New Testament book for each description below:

1. Luke's second book

2. A very action-oriented Gospel

3. A very Jewish Gospel

4. Paul's prison epistle which holds up the greatness of the church

5. Paul's prison epistle which holds up the greatness of Jesus as the mediator between God and man

6. Much like 1 Timothy—Paul tells a man how to pastor churches

7. The second of Paul's two letters to a region—in the first letter he had written an account of Jesus' second coming, but as a result they were quitting their jobs. So in this letter he tells them to keep working.

8. Paul's plea on behalf of Onesimus, a runaway slave who was now a Christian

9. A book containing seven different letters to the churches

10. A very practical word, practice must follow profession; the power and effectiveness of prayer

QUIZ THREE: GREEK

Transliterate the following words (that is, replace the Greek letters with each of their English counterparts). Then try to guess their English meanings. Refer to the Greek alphabet at the beginning of chapter 6.

1. ἀμήν
2. θεὸς
3. λόγος
4. Ἰσραὴλ
5. ἀγάπη
6. Πέτρος
7. φῶς
8. πατὴρ
9. πνεῦμα
10. Ἰησοῦς Χριστὸς

APPENDIX

QUIZ FOUR: HEBREW

Transliterate the following words. You should be able to guess their English meanings, though numbers seven through ten may not be as obvious. Refer to the Hebrew alphabet and vowel marks at the beginning of chapter 7.

1. אָמֵן

2. הַלְלוּיָה

3. דָּוִד

4. בֵּית לֶחֶם

5. שַׁבָּת

6. יוֹם כִּפֻּר

7. אֱלֹהִים

8. אֲדֹנָי

9. רוּחַ קֹדֶשׁ

10. יֵשׁוּעַ הַמָּשִׁיחַ

Answers to Quiz One:

1. Job (Genesis is written about an earlier time, but Job is thought to have been written before Moses wrote Genesis.)
2. 2 Kings (and 2 Chronicles)
3. Malachi
4. Exodus
5. Ezekiel
6. Genesis
7. Judges
8. Song of Songs
9. Isaiah
10. Lamentations

Answers to Quiz Two:

1. Acts
2. Mark
3. Matthew
4. Ephesians
5. Colossians
6. Titus
7. 2 Thessalonians
8. Philemon
9. Revelation
10. James

APPENDIX

Answers to Quiz Three:

1. Amen (in Greek this e is pronounced as a long *a*)
2. Theos = God (from which we get the *theo* of theology)
3. Logos = Word (from which we get the *logy* of theology)
4. Yisrael = Israel
5. Agape = Love (God's never-failing love)
6. Petros = Peter (also the word for *rock* from which we get petroleum)
7. Phos = Light (from which we get photon)
8. Pater = Father (from which we get paternal)
9. Pneuma = Spirit (also the word for *wind* or *breath* from which we get pneumatic or pneumonia)
10. Yiasous Christos = Jesus Christ (*Christos* meaning Messiah or Anointed One)

Answers to Quiz Four:

1. Amen (in Hebrew this *e* is pronounced as a long *a*)
2. Halleluiah (In Hebrew, *Hallel* is the word for praise and *Yah* is a shortened form of Yahweh, meaning the LORD)
3. Dawid = David
4. Beth lechem = Bethlehem (literally house of bread)
5. Shabath = Sabbath
6. Yom Kipper = Day of Atonement (in the Old Testament it was actually written as יוֹם הַכִּפֻּרִים = Day of the Atonements)
7. Elohim = God
8. Adonai = Lord
9. Ruach Kodesh = Holy Spirit (ruach means wind or breath)
10. Yeshua Hamashiach = Jesus the Messiah (*Yeshua* is actually the first century variation of Joshua, meaning God our help, or God our Savior)

BIBLIOGRAPHY AND BIBLE STUDY RESOURCES

Bible Commentaries

Of all the commentaries, no one series is best for every book of the Bible. If you were to get a series, however, *The New International* series is a classic, although expensive. The *Tyndale* series is less expensive, though quite good.

Fee, Gordon D., ed. *New International Commentary on the New Testament*, 18 vols. Grand Rapids: William. B. Eerdmans Publishing Company, 1984.

Hubbard, Robert L., ed. *New International Commentary on the Old Testament*, 22 vols. Grand Rapids: William. B. Eerdmans Publishing Company, 1990.

Morris, Leon, ed. *Tyndale New Testament Commentary*, 20 vols. Downers Grove, IL: InterVarsity Press, 2009.

Wiseman, Donald, ed. *Tyndale Old Testament Commentary*, 28 vols. Downers Grove, IL: InterVarsity Press, 1991.

Bible Concordances

Strong, James. *The New Strong's Exhaustive Concordance.* Nashville: Thomas Nelson, 1990.

Wigram, George V. *The Englishman's Greek Concordance of the New Testament.* Peabody, MA: Hendrickson Publishers, 1996.

Bible Dictionaries and Manners & Customs of the Bible

Chadwick, Harold J. and James M. Freeman. *The New Manners and Customs of the Bible.* Alachua, FL: Bridge-Logos Publishing, 1998.

Douglas, J. D. *New International Dictionary of the Bible.* Grand Rapids: Zondervan Publishing Company, 1999.

Packer, J. I. and M. C. Tenney. *Manners and Customs of the Bible.* Nashville: Thomas Nelson, 2003.

APPENDIX

Bible Software

Bible Gateway Searchable Online Bible. http://www.biblegateway.com. Zondervan, 2009.

BibleWorks Software for Biblical Exegesis & Research (8.0). CD-Rom. Norfolk, VA: BibleWorks, LLC, 2009.

Logos Bible Software 3. CD-Rom. Bellingham, WA: Logos Research Systems, Inc., 2005.

English Bibles

These come in various forms: chain reference, study Bibles, topical Bibles, life application Bibles, etc.

Holy Bible, King James Version. Public domain in United States, 1987.

Holy Bible, New International Version. Grand Rapids: Biblica, 1984.

Holy Bible, New King James Version. Nashville: Thomas Nelson, 1982.

Holy Bible, New Living Translation. Wheaton, IL: Tyndale House, 2004.

The Message. Colorado Springs: NavPress Publishing Group, 2002.

New American Standard Bible. LaHabra, CA: The Lockman Foundation, 1995.

Serendipity New Testament for Groups. Nashville: Serendipity House, 1987.

Interlinear Greek-English Bibles

Green, Jay P., ed. *The Interlinear Greek-English New Testament*. Peabody, MA: Hendrickson Publishers, 2005.
[Contains Strong's Concordance numbers.]

Marshall, Alfred, ed. *The Interlinear KJV-NIV Parallel New Testament in Greek and English.*. Grand Rapids: Zondervan Publishing Company, 1975.

Lexicons

Gingrich, F. W. *Shorter Lexicon of the Greek New Testament.* Chicago: The University of Chicago Press, 1965.

Mounce, William D. *Mounce's Complete Expository Dictionary of Old and New Testament Words.* Grand Rapids: Zondervan Publishing Company, 2006.

Vine, W. E. *Vine's Complete Expository Dictionary of Old and New Testament Words.* Chattanooga, TN: AMG Publishers, 1995.

Systematic Theology

Grudem, Wayne. *Systematic Theology: An Introduction to Biblical Doctrine.* Leicester and Grand Rapids: InterVarsity Press and Zondervan Publishing Company, 2000.

Theological Dictionary

Brown, Colin. *New International Dictionary of New Testament Theology* 4 vols. Grand Rapids: Zondervan Publishing Company, 1986.

Other References

Brown, Daniel A. and Brian Larson. *The Other Side of Pastoral Ministry – Using Process Leadership to Transform Your Church.* Grand Rapids: Zondervan Publishing Company, 1996.

Fisk, Randy. *The Presence, Power and Heart of God – Partnering in His Ministry.* North Aurora, Second Ref Press, 2006, 2012.

Ladd, George Eldon. *The Gospel of the Kingdom: Scriptural Studies in the Kingdom of God.* Grand Rapids: Eerdmans Publishing Company, 1959, 1988.

ABOUT THE AUTHOR

Randy Fisk received his Ph.D. in high energy physics from the State University of New York at Stony Brook. He also completed several years of graduate study at Concordia Seminary in St. Louis. He has taught at Valparaiso University and pastored with the Association of Vineyard Churches. Randy also spent a number of years teaching and leading worship in a church that is part of the Anglican Church in North America. He has spoken, ministered, and taught in various settings, always with the heart of empowering the people to do the work of ministry. Should you wish to contact the author directly, you may send e-mail to Randy at: RandyFisk333@gmail.com.

Randy and his wife, Mary, live in North Aurora, Illinois. They have three daughters, Holly, Becky, and Mandy, a son-in-law, Keith, grandson, Judah, and granddaughter, Rayah, all of whom are their delights.

Additional copies of this book, or Randy's first book entitled, *The Power, Presence and Heart of God: Partnering in His Ministry*, are available through online booksellers such as Amazon and Barnes and Noble. To inquire about multiple-copy discounts, e-mail the author.

www.ingramcontent.com/pod-product-compliance
Lightning Source LLC
Chambersburg PA
CBHW072335300426
44109CB00042B/1611